THE FOURTH ORANGE
AND OTHER FAIRY TALES YOU'VE NEVER EVEN HEARD OF

BY

HILLARY DEPIANO

BASED ON FAIRY TALES FROM *THE TALE OF TALES* COLLECTION BY GIAMBATTISTA BASILE

Copyright 2019 Hillary DePiano
ALL RIGHTS RESERVED

For inquires, requests for permission, to secure rights for performance or other needs, please contact Hillary DePiano through her website at HillaryDePiano.com. **Discounted acting editions are available for schools and groups ordering in bulk for performance or classroom needs.**

CAUTION: Professional and amateurs are hereby warned that this play is fully protected under the copyright laws of the United States of America. All rights, including professional, amateur, motion pictures, recitation, lecturing, public reading, radio broadcasting, television, and the rights of translation into foreign languages are strictly reserved. In its present form, the play is dedicated to the reading public only.

The author controls all rights, including the amateur live stage performance rights,. The right of performance is not transferable.

Copying this play either in print or electronically without written permission of the author is strictly forbidden by law. No part of this publication may be reproduced, copied, stored in a retrieval system, transmitted in any form by any means, electronic, mechanical, photocopying, recording, performing, or otherwise, without written permission of the author.

Due authorship credit must be given on all programs, printing, and advertising for the play.

Cover image by blendient.

INTRODUCTION

Believe it or not, this whole thing started because I was trying to put myself to sleep. I've got awful insomnia, which only got worse after I became a parent, and I was beyond exhausted and desperate for a way to actually fall asleep at night. By the time my doctor recommended reading something very boring before bed, I was ready to try anything!

So I tried the dictionary, tax forms, a vintage science textbook, just the most boring lines of text I could find. But, as Truffaldino says in the play, it turns out that reading something truly boring doesn't make you sleepy, it just makes you antsy which has the exact opposite effect. I needed something else. Something I'd been meaning to read for a while anyway.

I first stumbled onto Giambattista Basile's *The Tale of Tales* when I was in college. I was writing and directing an adaptation of Carlo Gozzi's *The Love of Three Oranges* as part of my honors thesis and wanted to read the original fairy tale Gozzi based it on. As soon as I started reading, it was immediately apparently that *The Love of Three Oranges* is not an adaptation of Basile's The Three Citrons as most people think but rather a mash-up of bits of several of the fairy tales from that collection, including the frame tale. If I really wanted to read the original inspiration for Gozzi's work, I would have to read the whole dang thing.

While that sounded interesting, I did not have time for that right then. I was already in over my head with school work and production woes while preparing to graduate. So I moved ahead with my Gozzi adaptation without ever reading *The Tale of Tales* because there just wasn't enough time.

But, over a decade later, I suddenly had time to read it since my evenings were so long and sleepless! And, hey, a bunch of weird old fairy tales would probably be just the right amount of boring to finally put me to sleep, right? But then they did the opposite. The tales sparked my imagination until, whoops!, I had a list of dozens I wanted to adapt. As often happens with writing, these collided with some half-formed ideas I'd had floating around my head about the grandchildren of Tartaglia and Ninetta from *The Love of Three Oranges* (which would be the children of Renzo and Barbarina from *The Green Bird*, another Carlo Gozzi play I've adapted) and the story of how Truffaldino met his wife and, before I knew it, *The Fourth Orange and Other Fairy Tales You've Never Even Heard Of* was born!

Writing this play was a true labor of love and the most involved project I have ever attempted. Beyond the historical research and multiple translations (Why, oh, why didn't I take Italian in high school?), I had three separate versions of each of the six fairy tales I adapted for this project and two different frame stories all housed in the same monster Scrivener file. In the almost six years this project took from idea to finished product, I spent a lot of time tearing my hair out while trying to figure out what I changed in which version, messing everything up, and begging my family and friends to please please please never let me write anything this complicated ever again.

But when I watched it all come to life at Rutgers Prep in November of 2017 where the cast and crew just absolutely knocked it out of the park, I knew it was all worth it. It was fantastical and funny and like watching these fairy tales step out of the shadows for the first time in centuries for another chance in the spotlight. I may not have figured out how to get to sleep but I did wake up something magical when I entered this fairy tale world that I can't wait to share with everyone.

ABOUT THE TALE OF TALES PROJECT

Giambattista Basile (1566–1632) wrote and compiled the 60 fairy tales within *The Pentamerone* (*Lo cunto de li cunti* in Neapolitan or *The Tale of Tales* in English) in Naples, Italy in the early 1600s. His sister, Adriana, published it in two volumes in 1634 and 1636 after his death. While not widely known, it's important historically because the Brothers Grimm later used it as the source for their far more famous fairy tale collection. *The Tale of Tales* contains the earliest known versions of fairy tales such as Sleeping Beauty, Cinderella, Rapunzel, Puss in Boots, Hansel and Gretel and more.

But I'm not interested in the stories everyone has heard of. I like the obscure ones, the weird ones lost to time. Why do we obsessively retell the same dozen fairy tales when there are plenty of other great ones we ignore?

It bothers me. So, since early 2013, I've been adapting these lesser-known tales for modern audiences to bring these stories back into circulation. I've modernized them with today's audiences in mind while still staying true to the spirit of the originals. Wherever possible, I also preserved the names from the original fairy tale and, where characters were unnamed, I've named them within the historical context and often with names from elsewhere in the Tales themselves.

This project is still ongoing. For the latest list of all the tales I've adapted from The Tale of Tales and what I'm working on next, visit HillaryDePiano.com.

Bibliography

Basile, Giambattista (2007). Giambattista Basile's "The Tale of Tales, or Entertainment for Little Ones". Translated by Nancy L. Canepa, illustrated by Carmelo Lettere, foreword by Jack Zipes. Detroit, MI: Wayne State University Press. ISBN 978-0-8143-2866-8.

Standalone One-Acts

Want to perform the individual fairy tales separately? There are standalone one-act versions of every fairy tale I've adapted from *The Tale of Tales*.

THE MYRTLE

30-40 minutes, 5 m 8 f (6-20+ performers possible)

A prince discovers his myrtle tree turns into a fairy maiden at sundown.

GOOSED!

(based on *The Goose*)

25-35 minutes, 2 m 6 f 8 any (11-20+ performers possible)

Two poor sisters rescue a goose that gives them gold but their sneaky neighbors want if for themselves.

ARM CANDY

(based on *Pintosmalto*)

35-45 minutes, 2 m, 4 f (5-7+ performers possible)

When a brilliant inventor builds herself the perfect husband out of sugar, he's stolen by a queen who wants him for herself.

THE FOURTH ORANGE

(based on *The Merchant* with characters from Carlo Gozzi's *The Love of Three Oranges*)

20-30 minutes, 4 m, 6 f, 5 any (7-20+ actors possible)

There were only supposed to be three oranges but Franceschina had to stick her nose where it didn't belong.

THE SHE BEAR

25-35 minutes, 2 m 2 f (4-10+ performers possible)

Is the prince losing his mind or has he really fallen in love with a bear?

VARDIELLO

10-15 minutes, 1 m, 1 f, 2 any

How much damage can one half-wit do before his mother gives him the boot?

Looking for something even more flexible?
Mix and match the tales above to create an evening's entertainment and I'll provide interstitial material and opening and closing scenes to connect the tales together no matter what combination you choose!

For more information about this custom option, email Hillary DePiano.

The Fourth Orange
and Other Fairy Tales You've Never Even Heard Of

For Mom and Dad, who always do the voices.

Photos by Scot Whitman, Rutgers Prep, November 2017

CHARACTERS
(In order of appearance)

LINETTA, romantic young princess
NICOLETTA, Linetta's sly older sister
RENZA, their innocent younger cousin
TRUFFALDINO, a once famous clown

THE MYRTLE

LA GIARDINIERA, peasant woman and talented gardener
BOOMING VOICE FROM THE HEAVENS
MIDWIVES
THE MYRTLE, Fairy by night, myrtle tree by day
KING MARCHIONE, Father of Prince Cola
LORENZO, Adviser to the royal family
VENDRAMINA, Social climber
MEA, Sister to Vendramina
DEA, Sister to Vendramina
PRINCE COLA, socially awkward prince
CHAMBERMAID
ROCCO, head royal gardener
GARDENERS

THE GOOSE

LILLA, poor peasant
LOLLA, Lilla's younger sister
THE GOOSE, sassy fowl of unusual abilities
PERNA, Lolla and Lilla's neighbor
PASCA, Perna's older daughter
VASTA, Perna's younger daughter
NEIGHBORS
PRINCE AMBROSO, prince of the realm, totally dreamy
BERNARDO, the prince's squire
MIRO, royal guard
MEO, another royal guard

PINTOSMALTO

ANTONIELLO, elderly merchant, Betta's father
BETTA, eccentric mechanicalchemist
IGA, Betta's lab assistant
PINTOSMALTO, handsome man Betta builds from sugar
QUEEN MENECA, Queen of Round Mountain
TOLLA, Queen Meneca's confident
SAMARITANA, old woman and blacksmith

THE FOURTH ORANGE

FRANCESCHINA, butcher girl, delivers sausages
CREONTA, fearsome evil witch, loyal customer
PRINCESS NINETTA, princess captured by Creonta, grandmother to Truffaldino's nieces
PRINCESS LINETTA, Princess Ninetta's sister, great aunt for which young Linetta is named
PRINCESS NICOLETTA, Princess Ninetta's other sister, great aunt for which young Nicoletta is named
PRINCE TARTAGLIA, lover of three oranges
THE GRIEVING GHOST, deceased purveyor of ghost nonsense
FAIRY PRINCE, currently being kidnapped
BANDITS, doing the kidnapping
THE SEXIEST GUY EVER, sexy guy with scary magic hair
RANDOM PEASANT, hapless bystander(s)
PRINCESS MENECHELLA, princess being fed to dragon
SPARKY, dragon with seven regenerating heads

A NOTE ON TRANSLATION

Throughout this play, I have used the spelling of names and places from Nancy Canepa's translation of Giambattista Basile's work with one exception. While Canepa translates the name of the handmade man in *Pretty as a Picture* (presented here as *Arm Candy*) as Pinto Smauto, I have used the alternate spelling, Pintosmalto, because it is more widely known and commonly used.

PRODUCTION NOTES

IMPROVISATION

In the spirit of the classic Italian theatre slapstick and commedia dell'arte tradition that inspired these adaptations, you're encouraged to put your own spin on all comedic bits and fights and to explore the physical comedy through improvisation. If you can come up with something funnier than the stage directions describe, go for it! I'm even happy to approve changes in dialog or more modern references, just run it by me first. For performer safety, avoid injury by always making sure you finalize all physical routines before the show opens. While you certainly don't have to, you're welcome to perform the show in masked commedia style if desired.

STAGING

Staging for this play can be as simple or as complicated as you want it to be. Because of the storybook nature of the tales, costumes can be anything from elaborate period pieces to paper bag tunics with just a few elements to suggest the character. Sets can be elaborately illustrated pages from a picture book, the crayon drawings of a child's imagination or a few furniture pieces where the audience's imagination does the rest.

CASTING NOTES

I encourage blind casting in all cases where it comes to race, gender, body type, etc. If you're in a casting pickle, please email me to explain your casting needs and I'll help you out. I can give you alternate character names and lines or grant permission to change character genders as needed, whatever we need to do to make it happen.

OMITTING A TALE

If you would prefer to shorten the play to perform without an intermission, I'm happy to grant permission to omit any tale but *The Fourth Orange*. Please email me and I'll provide you exact the cuts and changes needed to do that.

NEED MORE PARTS? INCREASING CAST SIZE

- **In The Myrtle:** While I've only specified two sisters for VENDRAMINA, the original tale has seven sisters total. If you'd like to get more performers involved, you may cast additional sisters named LEA, BEA, KEA, and ZEA and divide MEA and DEA's lines up amongst these roles. You can also increase the number of midwives, chambermaids, lords and ladies of the court, and gardeners as needed.
- **In The Goose**: You can get away with as little as two neighbors but the chaos of the scene is funnier with a bigger crowd.
- **In Pintosmalto**: While Betta's marvels can be props, they can also be performers that dance and sing as lantern colors and mechanical birds.
- **In The Fourth Orange**: Young Truffaldino and Franny can be different performers than Old as long as the audience can easily tell they are the same character. I've also only specified one grieving ghost, but the original tale has three. Random Peasant can be a single spokesperson for the crowd or you may divide those lines up between multiple ensemble members. One performer can manipulate Sparky, the Seven Headed Dragon, alone or a separate performer can play each head. (While the dragon has seven heads in the original fairy tale, you can reduce this number to three if it makes life easier.)

Please don't hesitate to contact me (hillary@hillarydepiano.com) for any reason. I'm here to help!

The playwright extends her greatest heartfelt thanks to the following groups who workshopped early versions of this play and individual tales. It is thanks to your excellent cast and crews that this show is what it is today!

SIERRA HIGH SCHOOL
JANUARY 11-20TH, 2017

RUTGERS PREPARATORY SCHOOL
NOVEMBER 16-18TH, 2017

THE PRAIRIE SCHOOL
OCTOBER 10 – NOVEMBER 4TH, 2017

ANNIE WRIGHT SCHOOLS
APRIL 26-27TH, 2018

SETTING
A fairytale kingdom.

TIME
The imaginary past.

ACT 1

SCENE 1

(Children's bedroom in the palace. This is suggested by a few easily movable pieces such as a distinctive bedspread, a colorful throw over the reading chair, etc. The princesses are all dressed for bed. Light music comes up from the ball downstairs. The oldest, Nicoletta, is attempting to play cards with the youngest, her cousin, Renza. Nicoletta's sister, Linetta, waltzes around the room with a bathrobe for a partner.)

LINETTA
Oh, Prince Robe, you're so light on your feet!

(Nicoletta slaps down her cards.)

NICOLETTA
Ha! Royal flush! Renza? Now you show me what you have.

RENZA
This card has a heart on it! So pretty!

NICOLETTA
You're hopeless, kiddo. It's not even satisfying to beat you.

(Nicoletta adds the last of Renza's stack to the hoard of cookies she's already won and then pushes the whole pile between them to share.)

Gads, I'm bored.

LINETTA
I wish they'd let us go to the ball. We're missing everything! The dancing, the music, the romance!

NICOLETTA
And all the good gossip. Grandma's probably drunk too much and going on about how she and her sisters used to live inside magic oranges and your dad used to be a bird or whatever.

RENZA
Did that stuff really happen?

LINETTA
I wish! No, sweetie. Grandma's just being silly. But anything is better than being stuck up here where nothing interesting ever happens.

(Truffaldino leaps into the room.)

TRUFFALDINO
Ta dah! Never fear, children, for you are now in the presence of the internationally famous clown, Truffaldino! Jester of kings, hero of magical quests, beloved comic icon and star of--

(The girls are unfazed.)

RENZA
Hey, Uncle Truff.

TRUFFALDINO
Not you too. Maybe I really am all washed up.

LINETTA
Why aren't you downstairs at the party?

RENZA
Yeah. Where are all the proper grown-ups?

TRUFFALDINO
Can't a guy come to visit his favorite nieces?

NICOLETTA
They kicked you out again, didn't they?

TRUFFALDINO
All I did was tell one, very tasteful, joke about the size of the King's codpiece--

(The girls groan)

RENZA
Even I know that's bad, Uncle Truff!

TRUFFALDINO

Comic genius is so often misunderstood. Why aren't you three asleep?

RENZA

Because no one came to read us a bedtime story, but now that you're here...

TRUFFALDINO

Oh, no no no. They sent me up here to make sure you're asleep so, go on, make with the snoring. The sooner you're out cold, the sooner I can go back down to the party.

RENZA

No story?

NICOLETTA

It's fine, Renza. Let him save face. We're used to a certain quality of storytelling and it's probably a bit more than poor old Uncle Truff can handle.

LINETTA

Nicoletta's right. It'll only be disappointing after the wonderful stories the nursemaids read us. They do the voices and everything.

TRUFFALDINO

I do the voices! I do the best voices!

RENZA

Maybe Aunt Franny can come and read to us! She's funny!

TRUFFALDINO

But not funnier than me, right?

LINETTA

Well...

TRUFFALDINO

No way! I've been a jester to Kings and Queens! I've left all the snootiest courts wetting their pants with laughter! I'm funnier than any nursemaid! I am definitely funnier than your Aunt Franny!

NICOLETTA
I don't know. The way I heard it, they sent you up here because you bombed big time.

TRUFFALDINO
You heard that from me! All right, fine, you manipulative little pests, let's do this.

RENZA
Yay!

(Truffaldino grabs an old book down from the shelf and reads the gold letters on the cover.)

TRUFFALDINO
How about... this one. "The Tale of Tales or Entertainment for Little Ones by Giambattista Basile." It's a collection of fairy tales.

RENZA
Oh! I love fairy tales!

LINETTA
Me too! So romantic!

(The princesses all start talking over one another and grabbing for the book.)
Can you read us the one about the princess who's trapped in the tall tower?

RENZA
I like the talking cat!

NICOLETTA
No no, one with action, like where the two kids get abandoned in the woods but the trail of breadcrumbs—

LINETTA
Oo, maybe where the evil stepmother won't let her go to the ball but—

RENZA
—and the princess pricks her finger and falls asleep—

(He shoos them all off.)

TRUFFALDINO
Girls! Girls! Ah, my head. Listen, I get to pick the story and I'm not reading any of those.

RENZA
Why not?

TRUFFALDINO
Because you've already heard those stories a billion times. There are thousands of fairy tales in the world. It's boring to only read the same dozen all the time.

LINETTA
But the rest are weird.

TRUFFALDINO
I got news for you, kid: they're all weird. You're just used to the other ones.

NICOLETTA
So what's your scheme? You're going to read us some stale old stories and try to bore us to sleep?

TRUFFALDINO
Shows what you know! A boring story just makes you fidget. But a good bedtime story grabs you by the imagination and takes you halfway to dreaming before you realize what hit you. You don't have a chance.

(He opens the book at random.)
Here! Our first story is called... The Myrtle.

RENZA
I love turtles!

LINETTA
He said myrtle. It's a kind of flowered tree.

NICOLETTA
Sounds thrilling.

TRUFFALDINO
Have some faith! I'm going to spruce it up a bit.

LINETTA
Spruce. Plant puns. Save us.

TRUFFALDINO
Ahem. Once upon a time...

(As he begins to read, the bedroom comes apart and reassembles into the setting for the first tale. Truffaldino and the girls can move freely through the stories unseen by the character in the story, coming and going as needed.)

SCENE 2

(La Giardiniera's cottage in the woods)

TRUFFALDINO
...there lived a woman with a gift for greenery called La Giardiniera. Her garden was the envy of all of Miano and the flowers she sold at market had no equal. But while her plants flourished, she longed for a nursery of a different kind.

LA GIARDINIERA
Oh, heavens!

TRUFFALDINO
She'd call each evening...

LA GIARDINIERA
Please send me a child of my own...

TRUFFALDINO
Night after night...

LA GIARDINIERA
If I could just have a little baby...

TRUFFALDINO
...she would plead with the sky...

LA GIARDINIERA
I wouldn't care, even if it was only the sprig of a myrtle.

TRUFFALDINO
Until one day...

LA GIARDINIERA
Come now, I beg of you--

BOOMING VOICE FROM THE HEAVENS
Fine! Your wish is granted! Just stop bugging us!

(She moves to the bed, straining with labor pains. Midwives flutter around her, getting ready for the birth.)

TRUFFALDINO
She grew large with child and, when it was time, the midwives watched astonished as she gave birth to a--

RENZA
A hedgehog!

(Bewildered midwives hold up a hedgehog.)

TRUFFALDINO
What? No! A myrtle!

(Midwives toss the hedgehog away and repeat the delivery, this time with the sprig of a myrtle plant.)

RENZA
But I like hedgehogs!

TRUFFALDINO
It was a myrtle. It's the title of the story!

NICOLETTA
Wait. So she gave birth to a tree?

LINETTA
That must have been incredibly uncomfortable.

RENZA
I have so many questions.

TRUFFALDINO
Well, save em. We're never going to get through this if you keep interrupting.

MIDWIFE
Congratulations! It's a... bush?

(They wrap the tree like a baby and give it to La Giardiniera who cradles it lovingly.)

LA GIARDINIERA
My myrtle. She's absolutely perfect!

ANOTHER MIDWIFE
Mmmhmm. Of course it is, lady.

(They snicker and exit. La Giardiniera plants the sprig in a large pot.)

LA GIARDINIERA
Pay them no mind, little one. Your mama loves you just as you are. There. Nice and comfy.

TRUFFALDINO
She kept the sprig in an ornamental pot and tended it with as much care as she would a human child. The tree flourished and tiny buds burst into beautiful flowers.

(La Giardiniera kisses the tree goodnight and settles into her bed. Night falls.)

Each day she brought the tree out to the sunlight and, each night, she brought it to her bedside where she sang soft songs to it until she fell asleep. Then one night, something wondrous happened.

LA GIARDINIERA

(waking)
What's that? Who's there?

(Gasps.)
Little one? Can it be?

MYRTLE

(unseen, a child's voice)
Mama?

SCENE 3

(The cottage, years later. The myrtle has grown into a beautiful flowered tree.)

TRUFFALDINO

The years passed happily until one day, the King and his court happened by on their way to hunt.

(The court trots by. King Marchione pauses in front of the myrtle.)

KING

Lorenzo! I've taken a fancy to this beautiful plant. I'll gift it to the prince when he returns tonight. Have one of the hangers-on grab it for me.

(He tosses Lorenzo a bag of gold and gallops off, the court following. Lorenzo pulls Mea, Dea, and Vendramina aside. They are dressed to seduce.)

LORENZO

Vendramina, you've made it clear you and your sisters seek the attention of the royal family. Here's your chance to win it.

VENDRAMINA

Oh, it would be an honor and our dearest pleasure to serve his royal highness in this or any other way he might desire.

(She lays it on real thick)

LORENZO
Yes. Well. I will, uh... Just see that it's done.

(Lorenzo exits.)

VENDRAMINA
A plant that pretty is sure to catch the prince's attention. Once one of us traps him into a marriage, the new princess can bring the rest up with her.

MEA
Well, then what are we waiting for? Let's swipe that myrtle!

DEA
But the King gave us gold.

VENDRAMINA
Which we'll keep as our tip. Come, quickly now!

(They grab the potted myrtle. As they disappear with it offstage, La Giardiniera appears in the doorway, disheveled from sleep.)

LA GIARDINIERA
Who's out here jabbering on while I'm trying to--

(She realizes the tree's gone.)
No! Gone? I won't rest until I find you! I'll run my feet bloody if that's what it takes! Myrtle!

(She runs offstage)

SCENE 4

LINETTA
Myrtle is such a weird word. The more you say it, the odder it gets. Myrtle. Myrtle.

TRUFFALDINO
Myrtle.

NICOLETTA
Myrtle.

RENZA
Myrtle. Myrtle.

(They all start playing with the sound of the word at once until Truffaldino cuts them off.)

TRUFFALDINO
Alright, knock it off. Anyway, La Giardiniera pursued as fast as her old legs would allow but the sisters were faster and soon stole the myrtle...

(The girls snicker.)

...the tree... back to the palace. That night, the King presented his son with the purloined plant. Prince Cola was so enamored with it that he carried the pot with the greatest care in the world into his own chambers and placed it in the balcony.

(The prince's chambers at early evening. Prince Cola enters carrying the myrtle, with Lorenzo close behind, and places it on the balcony.)

PRINCE COLA
Perfect. Sun and moonlight both touch that terrace so I'll be able to gaze upon it's magnificence whenever I desire. Look at it! Have you ever seen such a miracle, a jewel, the teardrop of an angel reflecting a beautiful dove.

LORENZO
It is lovely.

PRINCE COLA
Lovely? It's like looking at love itself. A miracle of nature, like dawn cresting a hill at sunrise, the moon full and glassy on a still lake, the eye of a falcon as it--

LORENZO
Your majesty.

PRINCE
I was doing it again, wasn't I?

LORENZO
You were going on a bit, yes.

PRINCE COLA
It's been a while since I had anyone to talk to.

LORENZO
I thought you handpicked your companions for this trip.

PRINCE COLA
I did and good fellows all, it's just that--

KING
(bellowing from offstage)
Where is that blasted robe? Lorenzo!

LORENZO
Forgive me. I must attend to your father. You know what he's like.

PRINCE COLA
Yeah, a royal pain.

LORENZO
It is good to have you back home.

(A woman shrieks offstage. The King bellows from offstage again.)

KING
Aha! Giving yourself an eyeful of the royal jewels, are you?

LORENZO
I must go. Goodnight, Prince Cola.

(He bows and leaves. The prince takes off his crown and jacket.)

PRINCE COLA
A bow even from one that's known me since I was a baby. I ought to

just prop this outfit up and wheel it out there whenever they feel like showing me off. There's not one of them that would notice. All anyone cares about is the crown, they don't give a fig for who's underneath.

(He can't stand to look at it. He tosses his jacket over the crown and heads to bed.)

SCENE 5

(Prince Cola plops down on his bed. Dusk becomes evening. The room is dark apart from a small bit of moonlight from the terrace. A figure starts sneaking across the room, dragging something. The prince jumps up.)

Ah ha! What's this? Some chamber-boy come to lighten my purse? Have at you!

(Blinded in the dark, he lunges at nothing and falls flat on his face.)

Slippery scoundrel!

(He dives again, this time coming close enough that the intruder yelps. He zeroes in on this, tackling her to the ground. They struggle.)

There! Now, to get a look at you.

(He lights the lantern.)

MYRTLE

Get away from me, villain!

PRINCE COLA

You're the one sneaking around my chamber in the middle of the night. I should call for the guards.

MYRTLE

Guards? Where are we? Where have you taken me?

(She tries to drag the pot to the door.)

I must go.

PRINCE COLA
Ah ha! You are a thief after all! That's mine!

(He goes for it.)
It's empty! What did you do with my myrtle?

MYRTLE
How dare you! I assure you, human, I belong to no one but myself.

PRINCE COLA
Human?

(He takes a better look at her)
Oh my... You're a fairy!

MYRTLE
I am. Do not pretend you are surprised. You knew what I was. Why else would you have kidnapped me?

PRINCE COLA
What are you talking about?

MYRTLE
The myrtle. You deny you stole it?

PRINCE COLA
It was a gift from my father.

MYRTLE
Then he stole it.

PRINCE COLA
Treason! My father would never... would probably not have... Actually, that does sound like something my father would do.

MYRTLE
I do not have time for this. The moon is already rising. Give me back my pot.

PRINCE COLA
But where is the myrtle?

MYRTLE

I am the myrtle.

PRINCE COLA

You're the myrtle?

MYRTLE

I was only a child. I had never granted a wish before. But she was all alone and so was I so, when they sent me, I thought... But I botched the spell. The plant and I, we are bound. It's too strong in the sun and it pushes me under. But moonlight is a time of magic and, while the tree sleeps, I live. It's only half a life but we made the best of it, her and I. You see?

PRINCE COLA

You're the myrtle?

MYRTLE

Are you even listening? Plant or person, fairy or foundling, my mother loved me for what I am and now she's all alone again. I have to get back to her before the sun rises and I'm rooted once more. Please, tell me the way back to the cottage in the woods and I shall be on my way.

PRINCE COLA

You're going to have to be more specific than that. This whole land is woods with cottages in them.

(She looks out the balcony)

MYRTLE

Oh, no! Our forest. It could be anywhere! What can I do? I will never find my way back home now!

PRINCE COLA

Please, don't cry. My father is like an elephant sometimes, trampling lives under his massive foot without realizing what he's doing. Whatever confusion has led us to this moment, know that I am hereafter your ally in setting things right.

MYRTLE

Even if you were the prince with all the power in the realm, my mother is just one person in a land of thousands.

PRINCE COLA
What do you mean? I am the... You don't know who I am.

MYRTLE
I do not. How can I know if you can even be trusted?

PRINCE COLA
Because I swear to you on the blood that pulses through my veins that I will do you no harm. You have my word on the sea that pools behind my eyelids when I think of your plight, on the fluttered wings of spring that dance in my stomach when I look at your eyes, on the heart that hammers against my chest like a lone apple trapped in a barrel as it rolls down a dew covered hill at the, uh...

(She's staring at him.)

Yeah.

MYRTLE
Your manner is strange. But I find that I do trust you.

PRINCE COLA
Then I will send for maps, scouts, whatever it takes to help you find your way home.

MYRTLE
Very well. Perhaps fortune will smile on us and I will not be away from home for more than a single night.

SCENE 6

(The Prince and Myrtle pour over maps on a small table in the prince's chambers.)

TRUFFALDINO
They began their search at once, but so much of the land was covered in the same dense forest of the kind the fairy remembered that the task seemed impossible. As morning dawned, they were no closer than they were at the start. It was the same the next night and the next. As the weeks passed, the myrtle despaired of ever finding her mother while

Prince Cola despaired of the day that they would.

(The Prince and Myrtle accidentally touch. They have a moment. It nearly becomes a kiss, but the prince's hand slips on the maps on the table, spilling them on the floor. They scramble to pick them up.)

PRINCE COLA

Whoops, let me--

MYRTLE

It's fine, I-- Oh!

(She stares at one of the maps.)

PRINCE COLA

What is it?

MYRTLE

It's... it's nothing. The sun is nearly up. I should get back to my pot before it rises. Forgive me, I must go.

(She exits to the balcony. Prince Cola watches her go.)

PRINCE COLA

Must you?

SCENE 7

(The next day. The Prince has passed out on the bed fully dressed.)

TRUFFALDINO

Prince Cola was exhausted, fulfilling his duties to the kingdom by day and working through the night to keep his promise to the Myrtle. When he did sleep, he slept fitfully, knowing the day their search succeeded was the day that he would lose the woman he loved.

(The King comes in like Boom! Prince Cola wakes so violently he falls out of bed.)

KING
Ha! They said I'd find your lazy butt still abed!

PRINCE COLA
Aah! Father?

KING
I grow tired of your sloth, boy! Since you're back, you've barely been in the court. You are the heir to the throne and I will not tolerate you shirking your duties. You're coming with me.

PRINCE COLA
But-- Ow! Ow!

(The King drags him out of the room by his ear.)

SCENE 8
(The court. Lord and ladies mill about. The King unceremoniously shoves the prince into his throne. Lorenzo brings Prince Cola some coffee but he falls asleep anyway. Mea, Dea and Vendramina approach the throne.)

VENDRAMINA
Your majesty, how we've missed your handsome face.
(He wakes. They have him surrounded.)

PRINCE COLA
I'm awake! I mean... Hello?

DEA
So tense, your highness. I could loosen those knots for you with a little massage.

MEA
No, let me! I've studied pressure points!
(They're all getting handsy. The Prince tries to escape.)

PRINCE COLA
Ladies, please. You're going to rip me apart.

VENDRAMINA
Wouldn't that be wonderful? If only we could tear you into little bits so we could each have our own princely piece.

PRINCE COLA
Uh...

DEA
Did you like the myrtle we got you?

PRINCE COLA
The myrtle? It was you? Lorenzo couldn't remember... Please. You must tell me where you got it.

VENDRAMINA
Of course, anything for you, your highness. It was from a flower seller in Miano.

PRINCE COLA
Miano! Ladies, I am in your debt.

MEA
Ooo! And we cannot wait to collect.
(The prince starts for the exit.)

VENDRAMINA
Oh, Mea, you've just given me the most wonderful idea! Come, we'll need some shovels!
(They exit. The King catches the prince before he can leave.)

KING
Where do you think you're going?

PRINCE
It's nearly nightfall, I must--

KING
That's it! There's only one thing you must do and that's whatever I order you to. There's a boar terrorizing the lowlands. And you're going to go and kill it.

PRINCE
Me? Couldn't you send some someone else?

KING
Of course I could! But it does the people good to see the crown running around shaking a spear at their problems. Makes the monarchy seem a little more real. Lorenzo, have them ready his horse.

LORENZO
As you wish, sire.

(Lorenzo exits.)

PRINCE
Now? But I've got--

KING
I will not be disobeyed! You're leaving within the hour and that's final!
(The King storms out.)

PRINCE COLA
The myrtle! If I hurry--
(He runs off.)

SCENE 9
(The prince's chamber. He races in.)

PRINCE COLA
I know where she is! Your mother! At last, we found--
(He checks the balcony. The myrtle is still a tree. He yells at the sun.)
Oh, hurry up and set already!
(He goes to the maps, pausing on the one the myrtle was staring at the night before.)
How can this be?
(The sun has set. The myrtle fairy enters from the balcony. He turns to her.)
The village of Miano. You already knew. Why--

MYRTLE
Because it would mean goodbye and I couldn't... I have developed

such an affection for you over these nights and I found I wasn't ready to part with you.

PRINCE COLA

You? For me? Oh, dearest fairy, can it be? For my love for you has burned like a fire made from a thousand suns, with a passion as hot as the bright red metal of a master-smith, and even so it is as strong as a thousand oxen each of them with legs of iron and a horns of polished--
(She kisses him.)
What did that mean?

MYRTLE

It meant shut up.

PRINCE COLA

Oh.

MYRTLE

But it also meant yes. I will marry you. If I wait for you to get to the question, we'll both be gray.
(They embrace.)

PRINCE COLA

Oh, my love! I never want to leave your arms!

(in the distance, the King calls him)

KING

Cola!

PRINCE COLA

Although, I actually have to go right now.

MYRTLE

Go? Where?

PRINCE COLA

My father is sending me on a hunt. For a wild beast that's terrorizing the kingdom, appropriately enough, since that's what he is.
(The King bangs on the door.)

KING
I heard that! Open this door!

MYRTLE
Oh no! How long will you be gone?

PRINCE COLA
I cannot say. But our party will travel through Miano. I can go to your mother myself and declare my intentions. My men will escort her back here in all the comforts of a queen so that you two may have your reunion.

MYRTLE
Then go. Complete your father's errand as quickly as you can and come right back to my arms.

PRINCE COLA
There is a chambermaid I trust. I'll tell her all. She'll see to it that you're watered and cared for.
> *(King bangs on the door again.)*

KING
Boy! I'll break it down if I have to!

PRINCE
I must go. He's not joking about breaking it down. It's already been replaced twice.

MYRTLE
I shall stay hidden until my mother arrives. We need a sign. This silver bell.
> *(There's a small bell on the prince's bedside table.)*

Tell my mother to ring it when she arrives so that I will know it is safe to reveal myself. Until then, my love, farewell.
> *(She disappears onto the balcony as the prince opens the door and the King topples in.)*

KING
Uff-- There you are!

PRINCE COLA
I was coming-- ow! You know, I'm a grown-- OK! OK! OW!

(The King drags him out by his ear again.)

SCENE 10

(As soon as the prince is gone, Mea, Dea, and Vendramina burst through the floor covered in dirt, with shovels, pick axes and other digging implements. They whisper, thinking Prince Cola is asleep in his bed.)

VENDRAMINA
At last! We're in!

MEA
So this is Prince Cola's bedroom.

DEA
Isn't he going to be angry that we dug a tunnel from our house all the way into his chambers without asking?

MEA
Nonsense! You saw how pleased he was with us today. He practically asked us to.

VENDRAMINA
What hot blooded man wouldn't want his lovers to be able to pop in for a secret tryst whenever he desired?

MEA
I should slip into bed with him right now and play at a little Mute Sparrow.

DEA
Wait. The bed's empty! He's not here.

VENDRAMINA
It can't be!

(She tosses the covers off the bed, overturning the bell

on the bedside table. The myrtle fairy calls from the balcony.)

MYRTLE
Mother?

MEA
Who said that?

MYRTLE
...my love? Are you back so soon?

DEA
There's someone out on the balcony.

(She pulls back the curtain revealing the myrtle.)
Who's this?

MYRTLE
Wha--?

VENDRAMINA
Some trollop sneaking into the prince's bed chamber hoping to seduce him in the night!

DEA
Absolutely shameful.

MEA
Yeah! That is our shtick.

MYRTLE
The prince? Whatever are you talking about? These rooms belong to my fiancé.

MEA
Fiancé? We're too late!

DEA
All that primping!

MEA

All that scheming!

DEA

All that digging!

BOTH

And for nothing!

(They sob.)

VENDRAMINA

Stop it! Pull yourselves together. She's lying. She has to be.

MYRTLE

How dare you!

VENDRAMINA

I've never seen you about the court, not even once.

MYRTLE

We were only engaged tonight, there wasn't even time to introduce me to his father let alone make it public before--

DEA

So, no one but the prince knows about you?

MYRTLE

Well, yes, but--

MEA

I'll bet I can make even him forget with a little game of Stone in Your Lap.

MYRTLE

Stay away from me. I don't like the looks on your faces.

VENDRAMINA

We've worked too long and hard for this prize to let you snatch it from us at the last minute, girl.

MYRTLE
Stop it. Don't come any closer.

MEA
No one will ever know you were engaged to the prince.

DEA
Not if you never make it out of this room alive.

VENDRAMINA
Tear her apart.

TRUFFALDINO
They advanced on the fairy, and she was soon overpowered. They pulled at her, each wanting to be the one to end her and, in their lust for blood, they tore her into pieces.

> *(They attack her. The more ridiculously gory it gets, the better. They can back her onto the balcony, so the violence plays out in shadows against the curtain. They freeze as someone tries the door.)*

MEA
What's that?

DEA
There's someone at the door.

VENDRAMINA
Come, quickly! Before we're discovered!

> *(They exit through their hole, covering it behind them. A chambermaid enters and discovers the carnage. She freezes.)*

TRUFFALDINO
The poor chambermaid came upon a gruesome scene: torn limbs, bits of skin, chunks of bone and teeth strewn about the room, blood pooling in... the... What?

> *(He stops. The princesses are staring open mouthed at*

the gore.)

NICOLETTA
Do our parents know you're reading us this?

TRUFFALDINO
Come on. It says right here on the cover, "Entertainment for little ones."

RENZA
How do you play at Mute Sparrow?

LINETTA
I think we might be better off not knowing.

TRUFFALDINO
Ahem, well, yeah so the girl rolled up her sleeves and got to work collecting body parts, scraping skin off the floor and mopping up the blood. Once she had gathered it all into the myrtle's pot, she gave the whole mess a generous sprinkle of water. Then she promptly ran screaming from the palace never to be heard from again.
(The chambermaid collects all the body parts into the pot, waters it and exits screaming as described.)

CHAMBERMAID
Aaaaaaaaaaaaaaah!

SCENE 11

TRUFFALDINO
By morning, the gruesome pile had transformed back into the myrtle tree, but it was a broken, dead thing.
(The next morning. Lorenzo comes to check on the myrtle. He discovers the dead tree.)

LORENZO
Ahh! The prince's beloved myrtle! Dead? Someone call for the gardeners! Oh, if the tree cannot be revived, he'll have my head.
(An army of gardeners file in with Rocco at the head. They puzzle and fuss over the myrtle tree as Lorenzo paces. Day turns to night and back again.)

TRUFFALDINO
He sent for the palace gardeners and they employed every trick they knew. As day turned to night again and again and the plant stayed the same lifeless stick, things looked bleak indeed.

LORENZO
This isn't working. Go! To the villages, the hovels, the farthest squat huts. Promise them riches, royal favors, whatever it takes! There must be someone in the kingdom who can bring this plant back to life!

ROCCO
You heard him, move out.
>*(Rocco sends the gardeners out and a new batch files in, which can be the exact same performers with more rustic hats. At the tail end of their procession is a hunched old gardener, her face obscured by her cloak. These new gardeners puzzle and fuss as more days pass.)*

TRUFFALDINO
Lured by the promise of riches, the best gardeners in the kingdom came to try their luck but nothing worked. One by one they gave up the task as hopeless.
>*(Gardeners give up and abandon the project one by one until the hunched gardener is the only one left.)*

LORENZO
Wait! Where are you all going? The myrtle! You must save it! There must be someone who--

ROCCO
They all gave up. Except for that one old thing that's been sitting there so long I'm not even sure it's still alive.

LORENZO
Yehk.
>*(He closes the balcony curtain on it.)*

ROCCO
You want my professional opinion?

LORENZO
What is it?

ROCCO
It's dead, yo.

LORENZO
My position if not my very life depends on reviving this myrtle!

ROCCO
Sucks to be you.

LORENZO
You are supremely unhelpful.
(With a shrug, Rocco leaves, passing Prince Cola on his way in.)

SCENE 12

PRINCE COLA
Rocco? What are you-- Lorenzo!

LORENZO
Prince Cola? You're, uh, back so soon!

PRINCE COLA
I found the cottage in Miano but it was abandoned, the garden wild and overgrown. I was suddenly overcome with a terrible foreboding. I had to return straight away.

LORENZO
Well, after so long a journey surely you'll want a wash, some fresh clothes--

PRINCE COLA
I want for nothing but to see my beloved myrtle again.
(He starts for the balcony, Lorenzo drops to his knees, begging at the prince's hem.)

LORENZO
Prince Cola, please, I throw myself upon your mercy. I know not what

happened and I have done everything in my power to try to repair it without success, but your myrtle is--
(The myrtle fairy emerges from the balcony.)

PRINCE COLA
There!

LORENZO
What?

PRINCE COLA
My love, I had such a terrible feeling of dread as I rode back but yet here you are.

MYRTLE
I was so cold. Those women they... Oh, my love! I had the most terrible nightmare.
(She falls into his arms.)

LORENZO
I have clearly missed something.

PRINCE COLA
The myrtle, Lorenzo. She's to be my bride!

LORENZO
You're marrying a tree?

MYRTLE
I am only the tree in sunlight.

LORENZO
You're the... But it... Ah. Prince Cola must have throttled me so hard when he found out about the myrtle that now I'm hallucinating. Yes, yes, let's just shut the whole thing down. Much better that way...
(He passes out.)

PRINCE COLA
Oh, my love, how I have missed you. I curse every blink that interrupts the viewing of your beauty. What kitchen lent the rosy red peppers for your lips? What sky is missing the shining orbs that became your

bright eyes? What sea waves sadly at the beach that held the shells that became your delicate ears? What master craftsman did shape your body like a--

MYRTLE

OK, you need to stop.

PRINCE COLA

Right. Sorry.

MYRTLE

I have read your stories. I know humans can be bewitched by our looks. But I need to be certain you care for me and not just the crown of soft curls. I believe you understand this well, Prince Cola.

PRINCE COLA

So you do know. I never meant to deceive you. It's only--

LORENZO
(wakes suddenly)

Wait a minute! The myrtle tree was dead! I had every gardener in the land in here, and they swore it was a hopeless case.

MYRTLE

You mean to say... it was not a nightmare? But then how--
(The hunched gardener comes in from the balcony.)

LORENZO

You! This is the one who saved the day, your highness. You should make her the new royal gardener because that other guy is the worst.

PRINCE COLA

If this is true, anything in my kingdom is yours, stranger, for restoring my myrtle to me.
(The hunched gardener reveals herself to be La Giardiniera.)

LA GIARDINIERA

I restored her to herself, young man.

MYRTLE

Mama!

LA GIARDINIERA

I have found you, little one. At last.
(They hug.)
So, you're in love with the prince, are you? Even without a monster for a father-in-law, you'll never have a moment's peace, not between balls and duties and jealous suitors. Are you sure you want to bind yourself to all that?

MYRTLE

Mama--

PRINCE COLA

No, she's right. About my father, the duties, the suitors, all of it. I am the man you knew in these rooms, but I'm also a prince with everything that comes with that title. I'm cursed too, in a way.

MYRTLE

I am not cursed. This is no enchantment to break. The plant and I are one, and that will always be so. This is my life.

LA GIARDINIERA

And it ain't easy!

MYRTLE

No, it is not. This is as normal as it can ever be between us.

PRINCE COLA

I don't care. That is what I wanted to say earlier. I am not bewitched. I love you as you are, fairy and flowers, inside and out.

MYRTLE

The good and the bad.

LA GIARDINIERA

That's how it should be. A plant needs both sunshine and rain to grow. It's just the same with love.
(King comes in his robe)

KING

What is all this blasted yakking when I'm trying to sleep? I'll have you all hung.

PRINCE COLA

Father! I'd like to introduce you to my fiancée.
(King thinks he's talking about La Giardiniera.)

KING

This old bird?

LA GIARDINIERA

Better an old bird than a gold boar.

KING

Ha! I like her!

PRINCE COLA

No, father, this is my fiancée.

MYRTLE

Your highness.
(She curtsies.)

KING

Oh. She's alright too I guess. Doesn't much matter to me so long as she starts popping out heirs in good time.

PRINCE COLA

Gah! Why are you like this?

KING

It's what I'm like, boy! Deal with it. That's the point you were all moseying around to in here anyway, isn't it?

LA GIARDINIERA

A seed grows what it grows. All you can do is your best to tend the plant you've got.

KING

See? Well, go on. You got us all up out of bed, now you two might as well make it all official.

(The prince and myrtle embrace.)
There! Now I gotta get the taste of all this sentimentality out of my mouth. I'm going down to the kitchen to yell until someone gets me some ham. Who's coming?

(All exit.)

SCENE 13

(The scene transforms back into the bedroom as Truffaldino finishes the story)

TRUFFALDINO
The lovers were married at once. When the new princess spotted Vendramina and the other treacherous sisters at the wedding feast, the prince tricked them into naming their own punishment and had them buried al--

(He glances at the girls.)
...a lot later in life... after some years in prison. Or something. Then they all, well most of them anyway, lived happily ever after.

(He closes the book)
There. What did you think?

LINETTA
Hmm. That was suspiciously passable.

RENZA
It was all story shaped and everything!

TRUFFALDINO
Ha! See? Now go to sleep, girls, and I might still catch a few appetizers before--

NICOLETTA
Hold on. That was one story. You really think it's gonna be that easy?

TRUFFALDINO
I... yes?

RENZA

Poor innocent Uncle Truff.

NICOLETTA

I don't think we've ever let anyone out of this room with less than a dozen stories.

LINETTA

And that time we only made an exception because Agnese was going into labor.

RENZA

But we still made her keep reading until the little head was peeking out.

(They give him a very innocent look. He is horrified.)

TRUFFALDINO

Okay... Well, what if I just leave? Say, "Go to sleep," put out the light, walk right out the door.

LINETTA

We'll follow you downstairs.

RENZA

You'd be so busted.

NICOLETTA

They already think you're washed up. What do you think is going to happen when they realize couldn't even cut it with a bedtime story?

TRUFFALDINO

You just said that one was good!

NICOLETTA

We said it wasn't as bad as we expected. Which means it was probably a fluke. No way you can do it again.

TRUFFALDINO

Oh, yeah? I'll show you! I can make any story in this whole book into a masterpiece, even...

(He flips through the book and points out a story.)

Aha! Here we go. "The Goose."

RENZA

Oh! I know this one.

TRUFFALDINO

No, you don't. Look, there are a lot of fairy tale geese but this one is closest to my heart because it's the most scatological, which is the only kind of logic I put any stock in.

LINETTA

So it's gross? Oh, brother.

TRUFFALDINO

Once upon a time...

(The bedroom comes apart and reassembles as the setting for the next tale)

SCENE 14

(A meager cottage. LILLA, waits by a small window.)

LILLA

Where is she? It's getting dark.

(Her sister, LOLLA, bursts in.)

LOLLA

Lilla!

LILLA

Gracious, Lolla, I was worried sick. What in heaven's name took you so long?

LOLLA

Here girl-girl! It's alright. Come on in. I want you to meet my big sister.

(A large goose waddles into the cottage.)

It's a goose!

GOOSE

Honk!

LILLA

I can see that. What's it doing here?

LOLLA

Oh, Lilla, please don't be mad. I sold the spinning like always but then there was this commotion and I turned just in time to see Prince Ambroso trot by and I had to watch him, just for a bit. Those eyes...Oo, they melt my innards like butter, and under his tunic, I could just about glimpse his tight little tushie and--

GOOSE
(appreciatively)

Honk honk.

LILLA

I've seen the lad myself and I am not immune to his charms but I fail to see what the firmness of the prince's posterior has to do with this beast eating the last stale crust off our plate as if it were another sister.

GOOSE
(offended)

Honk? Honk!

(It goes back to pecking at the hard bread. Lolla catches her meaning at last and cuts it in three, giving a portion to each. The sisters and goose share the meal as they talk.)

LOLLA

That's just it. I went to the butcher to get us something for the week ahead and I saw Goosey here in the pen ready for the block. She looked right at me with those sad little eyes and I realized that here I was mooning over the impossible dream of the love of a prince while all she wanted was to not end up as someone's supper.

GOOSE
(sadly)

Honk.

LOLLA
I couldn't just leave her to that fate, not when it was in my power to save her. So I brought her home to live with us.

GOOSE
(happily)
Honk!

LILLA
With all the money? Whatever will we live on until the next market? As if we're not struggling enough here without another mouth to feed.

LOLLA
Oh, she'll lay us some nice big eggs, you'll see.

GOOSE
(confidently)
Honk.

LILLA
But until then?

LOLLA
Come on, Lilla. Of all the things we don't have to spare, kindness is one thing we can certainly afford. It's magic everyone has the power to wield. Kindness is as good as gold.

GOOSE
(batting her eyelashes)
Honk honk honk...

LILLA
As if I ever stood a chance with the two of you making those big eyes at me. Fine, the goose can stay. Heaven only knows how but we'll make it work.

LOLLA
Yay! You hear that, Goosey! You can stay!

(She's jumping with joy and the goose joins her, flapping around and honking wildly as Lolla laughs.)

GOOSE

Honk! Honk! Honk! Honk!

LILLA

Alright, enough of that. It's late and there's a long day of spinning ahead of us tomorrow.

(Lilla gets into their small pallet bed)

LOLLA

I just have to make up a bed for the goose.

LILLA

May as well let her sleep here with us so she doesn't get too cold.

LOLLA

Oh, Lilla! Really? I told you, Gooseykins, she acts tough, but she's really just a big softy.

GOOSE

Honk.

(The goose settles into the bed between them, nuzzling up against Lilla until she gives in and pets her head.)

LILLA

You are a sweet little thing, aren't you? I'll tell you this, goose, you're no sillier than the sister I already have.

GOOSE

Honk honk...

(The goose sighs contentedly before falling into a rhythm of "honk-shoo" snoring)

LOLLA

Look at her little face, Lilla. Have you ever seen any creature so perfectly happy?

(yawning, half asleep)

My belly may be empty, but I feel full, you know? Like when you're so filled up with joy that anything is possible...

LILLA
Shh, silly girl. You're talking nonsense. Go to sleep. Goodnight, Lolla.

LOLLA
Goodnight, Lilla. Goodnight, Goosey.

(The goose makes a soft honk in her sleep. They sleep.)

TRUFFALDINO
Though they'd gone to bed hungry, they were happy and the three slept sound and warm. But the next day, they awoke to a surprise.

SCENE 15

(The next day. The sun rises on them all still in bed. Lolla starts.)

LILLA
Wha... what's that?

LOLLA
(waking)
Hmm? What is it?

LILLA
There's something cold against my leg...

LOLLA
Oh. Gooseykins must have soiled the bed.

LILLA
No, it's not that it's...

(She pulls the covers off and they gasp. Their bed is filled with gold coins.)

GOOSE
Honk!

LOLLA
Gold!

LILLA
Shh! You know the big ears next door.

GOOSE
(louder)
...Honk!

LOLLA
But there's a fortune in coins here! Where did it come from? It couldn't have just fallen from the sky.

GOOSE
(as loud as she can)
HONK!

(The sisters finally turn to look at the goose. With a flourish, the goose spins around and, with an elegant squat, poops out another pile of gold coins like those in the bed.)

LOLLA
Oh my...

GOOSE
(pushing the gold forward)
Honk...?

(Picks up a coin with its beak and handing it to Lilla.)
Honk.

LILLA
Solid gold fit for a King. It's a miracle! Enough to keep us in food for months. Lolla, we're saved!

GOOSE
Honk! Honk!

LOLLA
Oh, Goosey, you did this for us, didn't you? To thank us. I told you kindness was its own kind of magic.

LILLA
We ought to change your name to Goldie, you magnificent girl!

> *(The sisters embrace the goose and all three celebrate, dancing around and laughing and honking as the cottage scene goes dark.)*

NICOLETTA
Hold on. This is a story about a goose that poops gold?

TRUFFALDINO
Yup!

LINETTA
I can't imagine why this one never went mainstream.

TRUFFALDINO
The sisters celebrated as loud as they dared but then they set about keeping the gold quiet. They spent it carefully and only on necessities but even that was enough for their nasty neighbors to notice.

SCENE 16

> *(A few days later. The street in front of Lilla and Lolla's house. Their neighbor, Perna, sits outside with her daughters Pasca and Vasta. Lolla exits the cottage to feed and water their ewe.)*

PERNA
Lolla. Dressed for travel, I see. Where might you be off to on this fine morning?

LOLLA
Oh. Hello, Perna. Vasta. Pasca. We're headed to the market as soon as the chores are done.

> *(When Lolla isn't looking, Perna gives her daughters the signal and they sneak towards Lolla & Lilla's cottage.)*

PERNA
Again? You were there not two days before.

LOLLA
Well, uh...

(Lilla emerges from the cottage knocking into Pasca and Vasta who try to play it casually.)

LILLA
Come off it, Perna. It's just for a bit of thatch so the rain's not always coming in uninvited. It's not like we're off to fetch a bushel of rubies.

(During the following, Vasta climbs atop Pasca's shoulders with their version of stealth and peers in the window.)

PERNA
So touchy. What are you hiding, I wonder?

LOLLA
(too quickly)
Nothing! I mean...

LILLA
Oh, no you don't. You can just pull that big nose of yours right out of our business. Neither of us ever came knocking on your door asking why you always seem to have more than most despite never doing a day's work. Or why whenever something goes missing around here, one of your lot always turns up with one just like.

PERNA
I don't like the meaning between your words, girl.

LILLA
Then don't start calling another's apple rotten when all can see the holes in yours. Come on, Lolla.

(As they walk away, Lolla whispers)

LOLLA
I don't understand! We've been so careful. We've barely spent any of the gold.

LILLA
Shhh. Big ears.

PASCA
(whispering)
Well?

(Vasta mimes a rather abstract goose impression)
Are you having some kind of fit?

VASTA
(whispering)
Goose.

(Turns back to the window and then gasps)
What the... Aaa!

(Vasta screams as Pasca chucks her off her shoulders and hoists herself up for a look. Lilla and Lolla exchange a look at the sound and start back towards their cottage.)

PASCA
Let me see...
(looks into the window)
Whoa!

PERNA
(whispering)
Get over here, the both of you. They're coming back.

(They rush back to their mother's side. All three immediately try to look as innocent as possible as the sisters return.)

LOLLA
Is everything alright over here?

VASTA
Gold!

PASCA
...bye! Good bye!

VASTA
Uh, yes. We just wanted you to say goodbye to your gold leavings. I mean... Good leavings... to you... because you were, you know, leaving and--

PASCA
(covering her sister's mouth so the rest of her sentence is muffled)
Please, ignore my sister's verbal diarrhea. Um, that is... She's got the head of a goose on her and--

(With Pasca's hand still over her mouth, Vasta slaps her hand over Pasca's mouth. They freeze that way for a moment before waving innocently at Lilla and Lolla with their free hands.)

LOLLA
You two are so silly.

LILLA
That's one word for it.
(quietly to Lolla)
Come. The sooner we leave, the sooner we'll be back. I'm glad we got that lock for the door. I don't trust those two any more than their mother.

(They exit. As soon as they are out of sight, Perna, Pasca and Vasta drop the pretense.)

PERNA
Well?

VASTA
They've got a goose that poops gold.

PERNA
Hm. That's different.

PASCA
It's actually really disgusting if you stop and think about it.

PERNA
Then let's not waste any time thinking about it. Fetch my tools, girls! We haven't long before they return and that gold must be ours!

(Exit)

TRUFFALDINO
It only took moments for the three to hatch and plan and force their way into Lilla and Lolla's house.

SCENE 17

(A few moments later at Lilla and Lolla's cottage. The goose is napping as the three force the door open.)

PERNA
Where is that little feathered gold mine?

PASCA
There!

VASTA
Here goose goose goose...

(The goose awakens.)

GOOSE
Honk? Honk!

(Verna and her daughters all lunge for it but they end up falling over each other trying to grab it.)

VASTA
I've got it!

PERNA
No, I do!

PASCA

Get back here you stupid bird!

GOOSE
(defiant as she dodges all)
Honk honk, honk!

PERNA

Someone grab it!

(The sisters dive for the goose but collide into each other, knocking over Perna in the process. Pasca recovers and grabs the goose's foot, but the goose slaps her with its wings until she has no choice but to let it go again. Perna grabs at its tail as it retreats. The goose turns around and chomps down on her nose.)

PERNA

Ow! Aaa! It's got my nose! Get it off! Get it off!

VASTA

I'll save you, Momma!

(She starts to tug at the goose which only makes Perna scream harder.)

PERNA

Aah! No! Stop it, you fool! You'll make a ruin of my face!

PASCA

I'll handle this.

(Pasca is ready to slam a broom down on the goose. The goose releases Perna's nose and dodges at the last minute, so Pasca ends up hitting Vasta instead.)

VASTA
(getting pummeled)
Ow! That's me you're hitting! Stop it!

                        PASCA
Where did it go?

                        PERNA
            (nasally)
Over there!

            (The goose honks. They face off. Pasca armed with the broom, Vasta disheveled from the beating, Perna's nose gushing blood. The goose snaps her beak and raises her wings threateningly, think White Crane Style martial arts.)

                        GOOSE
Honk! Honk honk! Honk!

                        VASTA
It's a monster!

                        PASCA
Go and get it for us, mother.

                        PERNA
            (Clutching her ruined nose)
Certainly not. It's already developed a taste for my blood. It should be one of you.

                        GOOSE
            (a battle cry)
Hoooooooooooonk!

                        VASTA
It's charging!

            (They scatter screaming as the goose runs towards them, honking menacingly. It chases them all around the cottage until it corners Vasta and Pasca. They cower before it, and the goose gets cocky, showing off, snapping at them just to hear them scream. Perna sneaks up from behind and traps the goose in a blanket. The goose struggles but Perna manages to keep it

restrained.)

GOOSE
(muffled)
Honk! Honk! Honk!

PERNA
Quickly! Spread the cloths!

(Pasca and Vasta scurry to lay the tablecloth Perna brought with them down on the floor.)

VASTA
Our best linens? I thought we were saving these fine tablecloths for our dowries?

PASCA
What better way to enhance our hope chests than with a pile of gold?

(Once the cloths are set, Perna removes the goose from the sheet. They've got her surrounded.)

VASTA
Alright, goose. Let see those hind-quarters. Nickels and dimes too!

GOOSE
(a refusal)
Honk.

(Pasca gives the goose a rough shake.)

PASCA
Come on, you stupid bird, it's time to put the mint in excrement.

(The goose nips at her finger. She shouts and pulls back.)

VASTA
Something's happening!

(They all lean forward greedily)

PASCA

Here it comes! Oh, let me have it!

(With a grunt and a fart, the goose squeezes out a single brown turd. They all stare at it for a moment.)

PERNA

What's this brown lump? Some kind of trick?

VASTA

It probably just needs a little polish. Let me just...
(grabbing the turd, smearing it all over her hands)
Hm, ok, I really regret touching that.

GOOSE

(amused)
Honk honk honk...

PERNA

Stop wasting our time! We'll have what we deserve. Open up your bowels or I'll do it for you with a knife!

(The goose and Perna stare at each other for a moment. Then the goose squats again and lets out a stream of angry diarrhea that darkens the linens. The women recoil in horror and groan with disgust.)

PASCA

Ugh. That's foul, fowl.

(The goose examines the mess it made and honks proudly.)

GOOSE

Honk.

(She kicks dust over the stain and waddles off the tablecloth. As she moves, they notice the ruin of the linens.)

VASTA

The cloth! Our hopes!

PASCA

Ruined! So much for our future prospects!

PERNA

First my nose and now my best linens! You'll pay for this, goose!

(She rises, enraged, and grabs it by the neck. The goose is too surprised to even struggle.)

PASCA

Mother, wait!

(Perna wrings the goose's neck. It struggles for a moment and then its tongue lolls out of its beak and its body goes limp in her hands.)

VASTA

You killed it!

PASCA

But what about the gold?

VASTA

What about Lilla and Lolla?

PERNA

After the trick they've played on us? Let them think it wandered off.

(She tosses the goose's body out the window)
There. Into the alley with the rest of the trash.

(Vasta and Pasca stare at her)
Oh, stop your gawking. It's just a goose. Come on, we'll clean this up and search the place, it has to have left a few coins we can collect before they return. Let them come home to neither goose nor gold and see if that doesn't serve them right.

SCENE 18

(The street outside. Perna and her daughters sneak out of Lilla and Lolla's cottage, laden with gold coins.)

VASTA

Hurry! I think someone's coming!

PASCA

(peering offstage)
Is that the prince?

PERNA

Inside, quickly! Hide the spoils!

(As soon as they disappear into their house, the Prince enters with his squire and guards.)

PRINCE AMBROSO

Just a moment, squire. Nature calls and, from the smell of this street, no one will notice if I answer in that alleyway.

BERNARDO

Very well, Prince Ambroso.

(The prince disappears between the houses. There is some grunting that his companions try dutifully to ignore. Silence. Then a terrible scream.)

PRINCE AMBROSO

Ahh! The pain! Sweet merciful gods, make it stop!

BERNARDO

Your majesty? Uh, is everything alright back there?

(The prince emerges with the goose firmly attached to his bottom. It flaps and kicks at him from beneath his tunic, very much alive.)

PRINCE AMBROSO

No, you fools! This blasted goose has the soft of my bottom between its beak and won't let go!

MEO

What...

MIRO

How...

BERNARDO

Why...

PRINCE AMBROSO
(wincing and wriggling from the pain)
Aaa! I'd made myself a throne in that alleyway and finished my business when... Ow! ... I saw the freshly killed goose and thought its soft coat would do well for a wipe. But apparently, it wasn't as dead as it seemed. My poor bottom!

BERNARDO

That's what you get for wiping your butt with an undead goose.

PRINCE AMBROSO

What was that?

BERNARDO

I said, never fear, your highness, we'll free you!

(They begin to tug at the goose and prince both but the two will not separate. The prince bellows from the pain. A crowd is starting to gather as the neighbors come to see what all the fuss is about.)

PRINCE AMBROSO

Stop! You'll tear my tushie off. Aaa! I've never known such torment in all my days!

MEO

It's no use, sir. The beast has you like a vise!

PRINCE AMBROSO
(sobbing from the pain)
I can feel that, you fool!

MIRO
(drawing a sword)
I'll chop it off at the neck, my lord!

PRINCE AMBROSO
No! What if it stays clamped in death? Then they'll be no way to free me! Bernardo, plead with the crowd. See if someone, anyone, can save me from this torment!

BERNARDO
Peasants! Your prince needs your help with what I only refer to in the most literal terms as a royal pain in the butt.

PRINCE AMBROSO
Tell them I'll give them whatever they want! Riches! Titles! Lands! I'll... I'll marry their children! They'll get my hand and half my kingdom. Anything but this wrenching pain!

BERNARDO
You hear that, folks? The way to the prince's heart is through his bottom. His highness will marry whoever can get the goose to give up its puckered prize.

(All the neighbors start shouting over each other, pushing and arguing over who gets to try next. Bernardo and the guards try to hold them back but the crowd descends on the prince. It's chaos as they all try their remedies on prince and goose at the same time. All the while, the prince screams and sobs while the goose flails and flaps. In the midst of this carnage, Perna and her daughters come out of their house, Perna with her nose bandaged.)

VASTA
What's going on?

PASCA
What are they doing to Prince Ambroso?

PERNA
Hush, girls. Let's see how to use this situation to our advantage.

(They spy on Bernardo and the guards.)

MEO
What should we do?

BERNARDO
He said he wanted them to try.

MIRO
But they're not going to leave enough of the prince to marry!

PERNA
Marry?
(to Pasca and Vasta)
Well, what are you waiting for? Do you want to marry the prince or not? Get in there!

(The girls run forward into the throng.)
Hmm. For that matter, I wouldn't mind a prince to share my bed either.

(She joins the crowd. It's too much for the prince who flails like he's drowning before the crowd pulls him under. All that's left of him is a single hand above the mob and even that's still being beaten with a spring of rosemary.)

PRINCE AMBROSO
Help! Bernado! Guards! Someone! Save me!

BERNARDO
We're coming, your majesty!

MEO
Grab him!

MIRO
Save the prince!

BERNARDO
Out of the way!

(They disappear into the fray. At last, the crowd parts

to reveal the squire and guards holding the bedraggled prince aloft, bottom skyward, goose still firmly attached)

PRINCE AMBROSO

Get me out of here. Take me back to the palace! Perhaps the royal doctors will have some remedy for this iron jawed fowl.

(As they start to march him back towards the castle, Lolla enters and spies the goose. She drops her thatch and cries out.)

LOLLA

Gooseykins!

(The goose lets go of the prince and turns to her. The crowd falls silent. Now everyone is staring at Lolla but she only has eyes for the goose.)

GOOSE

Honk? Honk honk?

LOLLA

Silly, girl-girl. Whatever are you doing up there?

GOOSE

Honk!

(The goose flies to her immediately and showers her with kisses.)

PASCA

Ew. No. OK, you do not want to kiss that thing after where that beak's been.

(The servants lower the Prince who stares transfixed at Lolla and the goose.)

BERNARDO

If she's the goose's owner, your highness, we could try her for assault on--

(The prince holds up his hand)

PRINCE AMBROSO

With a word, her sweet voice did what potions and powders, strength and savagery could not. Look at her with that goose, Bernardo. I didn't think such kindness was even possible in this world anymore. I swear on my life that I would marry her even without the promise.

(He goes to her.)

What is your name, my dear girl?

LOLLA

Oh my goodness, you're the... L-Lolla. I mean, that's me. My name. Uh, your highness.

(She executes an awkward curtsy.)

PRINCE AMBROSO

Lolla. It rolls off the tongue like music.

(The goose steps between them.)

GOOSE

Honk, honk!

PRINCE AMBROSO

Is this your goose?

LOLLA

Please, sir, don't hurt her.

(She moves in front of the goose who honks defiantly from around her back.)

GOOSE

Honk! Honk honk, honk!

PRINCE AMBROSO

Hurt her? No one will ever harm a feather of that magnificent animal as long as I live.

GOOSE

Honk? Honk honk?

PRINCE AMBROSO

That goose has caused me a long afternoon of utter torment and yet I know now I would endure its grip a thousand times over so long as it ended with my meeting you.

LOLLA

I don't understand.

> *(Lilla enters, laden with more thatch, which she drops in shock as the prince drops to one knee)*

PRINCE AMBROSO

I promised to marry whoever freed me from the goose and you were my savior. Lolla, will you be my wife?

LOLLA
(overwhelmed)

I... Uh... I...

LILLA

By the stars!

LOLLA

Your highness, my sister...

PRINCE AMBROSO

Is welcome to come and live with us at the palace, of course. I'll find her a good match too if she likes. A gander for the goose too, while I'm at it.

GOOSE
(lewdly)

Honk honk...

PRINCE AMBROSO

The three of you should never want for anything again as long as you live.

LOLLA

I...

LILLA

Lolla, don't be a fool and keep the man waiting. Let him know your heart! She's been swooning over you for years, your highness, going on about melting innards and pert posteriors whenever you rode by.

LOLLA

Lilla!

PRINCE AMBROSO

Is this true?

LOLLA

It is.

PRINCE AMBROSO

It is a pretty great bottom.

(The goose honks appreciatively.)

GOOSE

Honk honk!

LOLLA

Oh, my dear prince. Nothing would please me more than to be your wife.

PRINCE AMBROSO

Then we shall be married at once! Oh, Lolla, when that goose clamped down on my cheek, I never would have dreamed it would be the happiest day of my life!

(the two kiss passionately as the crowd "aw"s and cheers)

PASCA

Ugh. And now she's kissing him with that same mouth. This whole thing is so gross.

VASTA

Hush. It's romantic.

PASCA
I guess...

PERNA
Come, girls, while everyone's distracted, we'd best make ourselves invisible before their goose comes to cook ours.

(They start to sneak away.)

BERNARDO
(leaning down to pet the goose)
What about you, little goose? Anything we can do for you for orchestrating this match?

GOOSE
Honk!

(The goose points out Vasta, Pasca, and Perna and they freeze. The crowd around them parts until they stand alone. The goose slowly mimes slitting their throats. It lets out a single vicious honk.)

Honk.

BERNARDO
Wow. Uh, OK.

PRINCE AMBROSO
You heard the bird! Take them away!

MEO
Yes, your highness!

MIRO
Stone cold. Remind me never to cross a goose.

(The guards seize them.)

PERNA
Stop this! I'm not like these peasants. I come from money. I demand to be put down at once!

PASCA
(overlapping)
It was self-defense! You don't understand, that thing is a monster!

VASTA
(overlapping, sobbing)
I touched poop... with my bare hands... for nothing!

(They drag Perna, Vasta, and Pasca out kicking and protesting.)

PRINCE AMBROSO
(scooping Lolla up into his arms)
Come, Lolla, Princess of Kindness. Let me take you and your sisters, both flesh and feathered, to the palace and your new life as my bride.

LOLLA
Oh, Prince Ambroso!

(To Lilla)
His eyes are even better up close! And the rear view's not bad either!

(They exit, the crowd following. Lilla and the goose are the rear of the procession.)

LILLA
Oh, Goosey, have you ever been so happy in all your life?

GOOSE
Honk!

(The goose squats, dropping a massive gold brick onto the ground with a clunk. Lilla picks it up.)
Well, there's the dowry sorted anyway. Come along, you ridiculous creature.

GOOSE
Honk.

(They exit. The scene reassembles into the bedroom as Truffaldino finishes the story)

SCENE 19

TRUFFALDINO

And so the villains were banished for their treachery and Lilla, Lolla and the goose moved into the palace where all lived happily ever after.

(He shuts the book.)
There. I know you liked that one, you were laughing the whole time.

(They girls are fading.)

NICOLETTA

It was OK.

(Renza yawns and dips with sleep.)

TRUFFALDINO

Aha! A yawn!

(Nicoletta elbows Renza who starts awake)

RENZA

No one was asleep!

LINETTA

Of course not. She's just doing her facial stretches, right, Renza? We do them every night, to keep our expressions fresh for balls and royal duties. Like this.

(They all start making ridiculous faces as if stretching their facial muscles)

TRUFFALDINO

Mmmhmm.

NICOLETTA

Yeah, our facial stretches and, actually, now that you mention it, we forgot to brush our teeth so we should go do that.

(She leaps out of bed and heads for the door. Linetta and Renza catch her drift and are close behind.)

LINETTA
Yes! We'll splash a little cold water on our, uh, teeth and we'll be good as new.

(Truffaldino tries to block their exit.)

TRUFFALDINO
Now hold on, what kind of sucker do you think I am? I'll have to start all over again.

NICOLETTA
Dental hygiene is very important. You wouldn't want our teeth to rot and fall out, would you?

TRUFFALDINO
Well, no, but--

LINETTA
Do you know what they make dentures out of these days? Hippos. Sometimes walrus.

RENZA
Have you ever licked a walrus, Uncle Truff?

TRUFFALDINO
I... have you?

(They stare him down)
Oh, fine. You can go to the bathroom so long as you come right--

(They race past him)

NICOLETTA
Great!

LINETTA
Thank you!

RENZA
I will think of you every time my mouth doesn't taste like a walrus!

TRUFFALDINO

Walrus dentures, where do they get this-- Hey! The bathroom is that way! What-- Where are you-- Get back here you little pests!

(He dashes out after them.)

INTERMISSION

ACT 2

SCENE 1

(The bedroom. An out of breath Truffaldino shoves the princess in ahead of him.)

TRUFFALDINO
I played your game and you're caught. Now get back in there you half-pint fugitives. Back to bed with you.

RENZA
Wasn't that fun, Uncle Truff?

TRUFFALDINO
Fun? That was a near death experience! You little monsters nearly killed me with that stunt.

LINETTA
You don't enjoy a jog in the brisk evening air?

TRUFFALDINO
Across the parapets with nothing but slippery castle stones between me and the big splat? No. No I do not.

NICOLETTA
Well, I'm not even a little bit sleepy now.

TRUFFALDINO
Oh, we'll see about that. I've been playing it safe so far but now it's time to find something with a little more zap to take you right to the Z's.

(He pages through the book)
Here we go. This one's called Pintosmalto.

LINETTA
I've never even heard of that.

TRUFFALDINO
Uh yeah, that's the theme of the evening. Do try to keep up.

SCENE 2

(Betta's room which she's turned into a workshop. Tools and bits of inventions are everywhere.)

TRUFFALDINO

Once upon there was an aging merchant whose only child was a brilliant beauty called Betta. But while there was no shortage of suitors vying for her hand, Betta turned them all away.

(Betta enters to put the finishing touches on an elaborate set-up of wires, bubbling potions and sparking gizmos all connected to something hidden by a sheet that lays atop her worktable. Her aesthetic is 17th mad scientist. There are improvised steampunk-esqu goggles a top her head and she wears a grease stained work apron charred at the edges. Antoniello follows her in, mid conversation.)

ANTONIELLO

Why are you so opposed to choosing a husband? I thought you liked the goldsmith boy, but you barely gave him a minute before you sent him away like all the others. He said you were as lovely as a jewel.

BETTA

Ha! I'll bet he did. A man who twists perfectly good metal into a useless bauble for his wrist wants a wife that's much the same.

ANTONIELLO

I'm only thinking of you, child. I won't live forever. I can't bear to think of you all alone with just your chemicals and clockwork.

BETTA

Oh, Papa. Have a little faith in your daughter's wits and give the order to begin the preparations. I will marry within a fortnight.

ANTONIELLO

Very well, my dear. But my heart is too old for all this mystery.

(He exits as Betta's assistant, Iga, enters.)

BETTA

It's not mystery, but brains and some good old mechanicalchemy! Ah, Iga, you're just in time! Let's get to work!

IGA

Yes, mistress!

(Betta removes the sheet to reveal the unfinished figure of a man.)

SCENE 3

TRUFFALDINO

While her father ordered preparations for the wedding, Betta went to work on the groom. She mixed half a qunintal of Palermo sugar and the same of almond paste with five flasks of rose water and cologne until she had a kind of sweet smelling dough. Then, with a silver scalpel, she molded rippling muscles and fine features until she had the figure of a man. Now he lay out on a table, where she was twirling him a magnificent mane of hair out of threads of spun gold.

(Betta puts the finishing touches on the figure lying on her work table. Betta assembles the face as Truffaldino narrates. Iga assists.)

TRUFFALDINO

Once she was satisfied with his body, she made him eyes from sapphires, lips of rubies and lined two neat rows of twenty pearls each for his teeth. When she finally stepped back to admire her work, the man didn't just smell good enough to eat, he was as handsome as a god.

(Thunder. A storm begins outside)

BETTA

Ah, the storm! There's no time to lose! Iga! To your position! Secure the rods!

(Betta and Iga suit up in protective gear and secure a crude lightning rod to the outside of the windows. Betta attaches wires to the body as Iga slowly cranks a wheel.

Outside, the storm rages. Lighting flashes inside and out while the current courses through the body on the table. It begins to twitch. Betta flips a large switch. Think 17th Century steampunk Frankenstein.)

It's working! We need more! Faster!

                    IGA

Yes, mistress! Faster! Faster!

(Iga turns the wheel faster and now the body is really moving, bouncing up off the table and groaning.)

                    BETTA

Yes! It's moving! It's alive. It's alive! IT'S ALIVE!

(She cackles maniacally.)

SCENE 4

                    LINETTA

Wait a minute.

(The Betta scene freezes, mid cackle.)

                    TRUFFALDINO

What?

                    NICOLETTA

Give me that.

(Nicoletta grabs the book from Truffaldino.)

                    TRUFFALDINO

Hey!

                    RENZA

Why are we stopping? It was just getting good!

                    NICOLETTA

Because he's making this one up. He's got to be.

TRUFFALDINO
I am not!

LINETTA
You really expect us to believe this scene happens in an Italian fairy tale written in the 1600s?

TRUFFALDINO
See for yourself!

(Nicoletta and Linetta scan the page. They look at each other and then Truffaldino.)
OK, so I may have added some lighting.

RENZA
Well?

(Linetta & Nicoletta exchange a look)

NICOLETTA
We'll allow it.

(She hands the book back)

TRUFFALDINO
Ha!

RENZA
Now can we please get back to the story?

LINETTA
Alright. But we've got our eye on you.

TRUFFALDINO
As I was saying...

(the scene unfreezes)

SCENE 5

BETTA
We've done it, Iga! The figure! It lives!

(The figure, now Pintosmalto, rises from the table slowly.)

IGA

In the name of the gods!

BETTA

Shh! It speaks!

PINTOSMALTO

Lady. Pretty lady.

BETTA

Oh, aren't you a dear. I shall call you Pintosmalto for you're as pretty as a picture.

PINTOSMALTO

Pintosmalto.

(He climbs down from the table and takes a few stiff legged steps towards them, arms outstretched. Iga screams.)

BETTA

Keep hold of your senses, girl. Why do you think I crafted him from sweets? He's as gentle as a kitten. Aren't you, sugar?

PINTOSMALTO

Nice Lady.

(He gives her a stiff armed hug. Iga flees, screaming. She nearly collides with Antoniello as he runs in.)

ANTONIELLO

Iga? Betta! Is everything alright? I heard screaming!

BETTA

Everything is wonderful, Papa! You're just in time! There's someone I'd like you to meet. Pintosmalto, this is my father, Antoniello.

PINTOSMALTO

Nice Lady's Papa. Nice Papa.

(He pats Antoniello on the head)

ANTONIELLO

Um, yes, well, it's nice to uh... Oh!

(Offers his hand to shake. Pintosmalto grabs it and shakes so vigorously Antoniello nearly falls over.)

Betta? What is the meaning of this? Who is this unusual man?

BETTA

Papa, this is my fiance! I've chosen a husband at last, just as you always wished!

PINTOSMALTO

Yay!

ANTONIELLO

I see. Do I want to know where he came from?

BETTA

Probably not. Iga, you get the crank and I'll-- Iga? Where has that girl gone off to?

PINTOSMALTO

Pinto help!

(He yanks the crank off the wall)

BETTA

Nu uh uh! Pinto can help by just standing there and giving Nice Lady something handsome to look at. Don't you worry your pretty little head about any of this.

(She twists a bit of wire into a flower shape and hands it to him)

PINTOSMALTO

Oh. OK. Pinto just stand here with pretty head. Pinto stay out Nice Lady's way.

(He tucks the wire flower behind his ear and grins at her.)

BETTA
You see? He's perfect. I'm in love, Papa.

ANTONIELLO
Well, I suppose that's all there is to it. Come, lad. We'll have you fit for some proper clothes. The wedding day will be here before we know it.

(all exit)

SCENE 6

TRUFFALDINO
Soon Betta and her handmade groom were married. Guests from all along her father's trade route came to celebrate the wedding with days of food and dance. But not everyone who attended wished them well.

(Antoniello and Betta's home. Sounds of dancing offstage. Queen Meneca and her confidant Tolla confer in private.)

QUEEN MENECA
This disgusting place. Everywhere, nothing but commoners and their dusty little lives. My dear Tolla, how I long for the gleam of my own court.

TOLLA
Then we should take our leave, Queen Meneca.

QUEEN MENECA
Nonsense. I came all this way. I refuse to return empty bedded. After all those years with that withered old husk of a husband, don't I deserve a little arm candy? Oh! Hush. He's coming and alone for once. Now is my chance. See that the carriage is ready to leave at a moment's notice.

TOLLA
As you wish. Happy hunting, my queen!

(Tolla exits. Pintosmalto enters dressed for the wedding, wire flower still behind his ear. He executes an awkward bow.)

PINTOSMALTO
Is late, Fancy Lady. Nice Lady ask Pinto show you to room.

QUEEN MENECA
Why, yes, that would be perfect! My room is in my castle at Round Mountain. Won't you show me there?

PINTOSMALTO
Pinto will. Make Nice Lady proud!

QUEEN MENECA
Oh, I'm sure she'll be absolutely delighted.

(Unnoticed, she plucks the wire flower and tosses it on the ground. They exit.)

TRUFFALDINO
Pintosmalto was new to this world and knew nothing of treachery, so he went willingly, thinking he was doing his duty, even as the Queen shoved him into her carriage and tore off towards Round Mountain.

(Betta enters)

BETTA
Husband! Pintosmalto? Where has he gotten off to?

(She finds the discarded flower.)
He's gone? Unacceptable.

(She starts to go, passing her father.)

ANTONIELLO
Betta, there are some people I'd like you to-- What is it? Where are you going?

BETTA
I go to collect what's mine.

ANTONIELLO
But--

(She's already left. He pursues her.)

Betta? Wait! Child, no, don't go, I beg of you!

(Exit)

SCENE 7

TRUFFALDINO

Though her father pleaded himself sick, Betta would not be deterred. With only a traveling cloak, a few supplies and a head full of wits, she set out at once to find Pintosmalto. The journey was long and hard. Her father's trade route wound across the land and weeks of searching stretched into months as the season grew cold and cruel.

> *(Betta trudges, huddling against the cold. She struggles against the snow and wind that rushes all around her.)*

BETTA

So cold... If only I could rest for... No. To stop here would be death so I must... I must...

> *(She finally falls from sheer exhaustion. With the last of her strength, she lights a beacon that projects a burst of colors)*

TRUFFALDINO

At last, Betta could not go on. She'd rigged up an emergency beacon, a lantern that burned in fantastical colors that she hoped would attract some aide. She had just enough strength to activate it before the cold entered her bones and the world went dark.

> *(An old woman, Samaritana, comes to investigate the beacon and discovers Betta, barely conscious. She pulls Betta to her feet and guides her to her blacksmith shop.)*

She was barely alive when strong hands pulled her to her feet. Her savior was a blacksmith and as Betta defrosted by her forge, she told her everything.

BETTA

...but I'd have turned back months ago were it not for more recent complications.

(She removes her cloak to reveal that she is heavily pregnant.)

SAMARITANA
God's teeth. You're pregnant.

BETTA
Such a blasted inconvenience! Now I'll be ruined by gossips if I return without my husband. My father is old enough, the shock could kill him! But I fear I've risked everything for another dead end. The last name on my list is a great Queen.

SAMARITANA
Ha! Queen Meneca is only great the way you'd call a plague so. Now that you say it, she did come home a few months ago with a dazzling man, eyes like gems, features like they were carved from marble.

BETTA
That's my Pintosmalto! Please, take me to him at once.

SAMARITANA
Oh, lass. You're too late. He's forgotten you. She's married him herself.

BETTA
No. I will not accept it. I only need a moment with him, and he'll return to me at once, I'm certain of it.

SAMARITANA
Very well. But she keeps the man as she does all her beautiful things: Locked away for no eyes but her own. They say she's got quite a collection of treasures hidden away. She'd go mad for this lantern of yours.

BETTA
My beacon? But it's just a simple chemical reaction.

SAMARITANA
She wouldn't care about anything other than it's pretty and no one else has its like.

BETTA

Hmm. You put me in mind of a plan.

SAMARITANA

Then count me in. I have no love for Queen Meneca. If your happiness comes at her misery, I'm happy to lend my fire to that service.

> *(They shake on it and confer in pantomime during the narration)*

TRUFFALDINO

Within an hour of plotting, the women were as close as friends of a lifetime. When she finally relented to a much-needed rest, Betta was confident that her happy ending began on the morrow.

> *(Exit)*

SCENE 8

> *(Queen Meneca's castle. Queen Meneca paces. Outside the window, Betta's lantern puts on a colorful show.)*

TRUFFALDINO

The next night, colored lights danced against the walls of Queen Meneca's castle. The Queen was nearly in fits with desire for the source of the beautiful show when Tolla lead two mysterious travelers, who were really Betta and Samaritana in disguise, into her throne room.

> *(Tolla leads Betta and Samaritana, both disguised, in with the beacon. The beacon transforms the room with its colorful lights.)*

They arranged a trade. The lantern for an evening alone outside Pintosmalto's bedchamber.

> *(Meneca leads Betta to the door of Pintosmalto's bed chamber. Betta hands her the lantern. As soon as the queen leaves, Betta runs to the keyhole and starts calling through it.)*

BETTA

Pintosmalto? Oh, if you knew the trials I've undergone just to find you but there's no time, we've got to get you out of here so smash down this door before-- Pintosmalto? Hello? Why in heaven won't you look at me?

(She keeps trying to wake him as Truffaldino narrates)

TRUFFALDINO

But when Betta arrived for her reward, no matter how she called through the keyhole or pounded on the door, Pintosmalto never showed any sign of hearing her at all. When the sun peaked over the horizon, Queen Meneca found Betta still whispering herself hoarse, beating her fists raw against the door.

(Morning. Queen Meneca enters)

QUEEN MENECA

Your time is up. I trust your reward was everything you hoped it would be.

BETTA

What? No! This is an outrage! He never even---

QUEEN MENECA

Oh, dear. You aren't going to prove troublesome, are you? I'd hate to have my guards make an example of you in the square.

BETTA

(quickly adopts disguised voice)
Ah, no. No trouble here, your majesty. I will go.

(to herself)
But I will be back. With a treasure that makes that lantern look like a chamber pot.

(Exits.)

SCENE 9

(Queen Menca's castle)

TRUFFALDINO
Betta and Samaritana returned to the forge and worked day and night until they'd come up with a new marvel to tempt the queen. Soon, an enchanting melody floated up to Queen Meneca until she could bare it no more and sent Tolla to make it hers.

> *(Tolla leads in Betta and Samaritana disguised. They wheel in a covered bird cage.)*

TOLLA
Queen Meneca, these minstrels have come to demonstrate their musical marvel.

QUEEN MENECA
Minstrels? Then where are their instruments?

TRUFFALDINO
Without a word, the minstrels, who were really Betta and Samaritana in a new disguise, pulled back the cloth and revealed a bird cage ringed in bells that rang on their own while mechanical birds harmonized and danced on their perches.

> *(As Truffaldino describes it, the bird cage comes alive with dancing birds tweeting and bells tinkling out a beautiful tune. It can be a current pop hit for the anachronistic comedy value.)*

Queen Meneca had to have it. So they arranged another trade.

QUEEN MENECA
...for an another evening with Pintosmalto. You can wait outside his bedchamber again--

BETTA
No. I will meet him here and now, no doors between us.

QUEEN MENECA
Oh, very well. Just get my beautiful birds safely into my treasure room, and I'll send for Pintosmalto.

> *(Betta and Samaritana exit with cage.)*

Pintosmalto! Come down here at once!

TOLLA
But, Meneca, unchaperoned, not even a door to--

QUEEN MENECA
We'll repeat our trick, pay the fare in bad coin. What's the harm to us?

TOLLA
None, I suppose. I'll prepare the wine.

(Tolla exits as Pintosmalto enters, dressed royally)

QUEEN MENECA
There you are, husband. These fine clothes do suit you. I can never tire of looking at your handsome figure.

PINTOSMALTO
Pinto's butt itches.

QUEEN MENECA
But then you always go and spoil it.

PINTOSMALTO
Pinto come cause Fancy Lady--

QUEEN MENECA
Do shut your mouth. I'm in no mood for your prattle.

(Tolla returns with the wine)
Thank you, Tolla. Down this.

PINTOSMALTO
But wine make Pinto sleepy. Give Pinto weird dreams.

QUEEN MENECA
You dare argue with me, your Queen? Drink it! Now.

PINTOSMALTO
Pinto shut mouth.

(He drinks the wine and sits. Betta enters. Pinto yawns, drooping.)

QUEEN MENECA

You are just in time. We'll leave you to your reward.

SCENE 10

(Queen Meneca and Tolla exit. Betta runs to Pintosmalto, his eyes open.)

BETTA

Ah, Pintosmalto! They'll be no ignoring me this time! It's me, your true wife. She stole you from me and now you've... What is it? Are you ignoring me? Has it been so long that you don't recognize...

(He snores, his eyes closing. The sleeping draught in the wine has knocked him out completely.)

Asleep? No! Wake up! Please! You sleep but it's me trapped in this nightmare!

(She keeps trying to wake him)

TRUFFALDINO

No matter how she pounded his chest or shook his shoulders, Pintosmalto would not wake. When the hour was up and Queen Meneca returned, still he snored, oblivious to Betta's desperate pleas.

(Queen Meneca enters.)

QUEEN MENECA

No luck?

BETTA

How dare you! I'll have your neck, you--

(Betta lunges for her, but Samaritana rushes in and hold her back. Meneca laughs as Samaritana leads Betta out of the castle)

SAMARITANA

Shh! Patience, Betta.

BETTA

We don't have time for patience! The baby is coming! It will emerge any day now and Papa and I's lives will be ruined.

(Exit.)

SCENE 11

TRUFFALDINO

Day and night, Betta worked building a third marvel. As she grew ever more tired from her labors and labors of another kind yet to come, she knew she was running out of time. The baby was coming, and this was her very last chance.

(Queen Meneca's castle. Queen Meneca is at leisure when Betta busts in, pursued by Tolla.)

TOLLA

I couldn't stop her. She just barreled through the door! I'll call the guards, have them--

QUEEN MENECA

Not yet. Have you brought me another present, silly girl? I do so enjoy watching you waste these treasures on hopeless chances.

BETTA

I have no patience for chatter. Let's get down to it.

TRUFFALDINO

Betta whistled and a cart set for tea wheeled itself in. She whistled again and the cart began to dance, rolling around the room in lovely patterns, until it finally stopped in front of Queen Meneca. She gasped in delight when mechanical hands rose up from the cart and served her tea and sandwiches.

(The tea cart dances and serves tea as described.)

BETTA

There. Now, do you want it or not?

QUEEN MENECA
(nibbling a sandwich)
Hmm, yes. I believe I do.

BETTA

Good, this time I want--

QUEEN MENECA

No. I am done playing games, merchant girl.

(Betta abandons her disguise)

BETTA

So you admit it! You stole my husband! Bring him here. Let me talk to him. If I had but an hour alone with Pintosmalto, he'd be mine again.

QUEEN MENECA

Is that so? What would you stake on it?

BETTA

I've already shown you the cart.

QUEEN MENECA

No. This time I name the price. The cart and you. You to stay here in my palace as my slave, making me treasures like this every day. And when the child is born, you give it to me and go along when I say it is mine. I have no love for children, but they are profitable enough when you call them heirs marry them off nice and young.

TOLLA

But Meneca--

BETTA

Fine. I accept. It doesn't matter what the price is for failure when success is guaranteed.

QUEEN MENECA

Wonderful! Then let us waste no time in settling our little wager. Bring my cart to the treasure room, and we'll begin at once. Pintosmalto! Come down here! Tolla, go and fetch my husband a drink. I'm sure they'll have much to discuss, and I'd hate for his throat to be too parched for conversation.

(Betta exits with the cart and misses the obvious wink Meneca gives Tolla)

TOLLA

As you wish.

SCENE 12

(Pintosmalto enters.)

QUEEN MENECA

There are you, Pintosmalto. It's about-- what's this?

(He's twisted some wire into a crude flower and tucked it behind his ear)

A bit of twisted metal. Trash.

(She tosses it. Tolla has the wine)

Sit. Drink this. And I don't want to hear any protests this... Oh.

(He's already downed it and plopped into the chair. He yawns as Betta returns.)

BETTA

Pintosmalto! Finally! Tell this woman that I...

(He snores, apparently dead asleep)

Asleep again? No! How? It's barely noon. How can this be?

(She sees the cup)

The wine! I should have known. You drugged him!

(Queen Meneca laughs)

QUEEN MENECA

What's the matter, girl? Finding it harder than you thought to win the man back? I wonder what lovely trinket my clever little captive will make me first.

BETTA

Villain! You cheated!

QUEEN MENECA

You may cry all about it to my guards. They'll be along as soon as your hour is up to drag you to my dungeons. But gently, of course, to protect my investment. I'm already thinking of several profitable options for that little brat just as soon as you pop it out for me.

BETTA
You will never lay a hand on my child, and I will never make you anything!

QUEEN MENECA
Then you can have your baby in the stocks and let the cold take you both for all I care.

(She storms out)

SCENE 13

BETTA
Oh, Pintosmalto! I've really done it this time. I should have listened to Samaritana, should have checked my foolish pride, should have made myself a husband with a face like a normal man instead of a god or she never would have... All those suitors that only wanted me to be something sweet and pretty on their arm and I wanted to show them... I wanted them to see that I... But then, I only did the same thing to you they'd have done to me. I am a fool.

PINTOSMALTO
No. Pinto not remember everything but he remember Nice Lady not fool. Nice Lady smart. The most smart.

BETTA
You're awake? But how can this be?

PINTOSMALTO
Two time wine make dream of Nice Lady. But Nice Lady sad and Pinto not hear what she say. So Pinto think like sneaky queen and switch sleepy powder with flour. Make bad wine taste. But Pinto stay awake!

BETTA
Amazing!

PINTOSMALTO
Pinto not fool either, only new. But understand now that everything not sugar and almond paste.

BETTA
Then we leave now and we start over.

PINTOSMALTO
But how? Fancy Lady has guards with pointy sticks! Horses run faster than Pinto!

(Betta strips the tablecloth and tea setting off the cart to reveal the gears and other workings below. She starts to tinker with it. The hands that served tea can help.)

BETTA
This thing can outrun any horse if I can just get it up to full speed. But it's not working right.

PINTOSMALTO
What this part do?

BETTA
That's the gear for the front wheels. They pull the whole thing forward. But they're not giving me enough power.

PINTOSMALTO
And what these pretty little wheels back here do?

BETTA
Nothing. Those are just decorative.

PINTOSMALTO
Oh. But could they maybe also help?

(She stares at him, then the wheels)

BETTA
Why, yes, I do believe they could. I could rig it in half a minute. I'd just need some wire. Where is that... Aha!

(She produces the original wire flower)

Blast! It's not quite enough. I kept this for you. When I thought you had forgotten me, I hoped it would--

(Pinto retrieves the metal flower he made from where Meneca tossed it)

PINTOSMALTO
Pinto never forget Nice Lady. Pinto feel her fingerprints pressed into his heart.

(He shows her his flower. They have a moment. Then both untwist the flowers and get to work wiring up the back wheels.)

BETTA
It goes around like this. Make sure you tighten the-- perfect! You're a natural! Now, give it a spin. Ha! Wonderful! This might actually work!

SCENE 14

(Queen Meneca and Tolla enter)

QUEEN MENECA
Well. I see you've played quite a little trick on me, husband. Though it won't do you any good. I don't care how clever the girl is, she can't use potions and bits of gears to make a way out. You're trapped-- Aah!

(She screams as Samaritana blasts through the wall behind her.)

SAMARITANA
Shows what you know! Nothing easier to make than a hole!

(Queen Meneca and Tolla are buried in debris, trying to right themselves)

BETTA
Samaritana! Hop on!

SAMARITANA
Alright, but I got a fair bit of luggage.

(With effort, she drags in a huge sack of treasure which includes the marvels Betta traded earlier)

QUEEN MENECA
My treasures! Thieves!

TOLLA
Guards!

SAMARITANA
Your guards are going to be a bit held up what with all the doors being welded shut and all.

(Betta and Pintosmalto finish the repairs)

BETTA
Got it! It's time to go home.

(Betta and Samaritana get onto the cart. Pintosmalto starts to get on after them.)

QUEEN MENECA
And where exactly do you think you're going, husband?

BETTA
Stop calling him that! Your marriage was a sham.

QUEEN MENECA
No, you foolish girl! Mine is the real one. A Queen's word is worth triple the one of a nothing like you. He is and will always be my husband because I say so.

BETTA
That is not how it--

PINTOSMALTO
Pinto is Fancy Lady's husband. Is real marriage?

BETTA
Pintosmalto, sweetie, no, she--

QUEEN MENECA
Yes. I say that you are bound to me, and it is so. There is nothing she can do to change that.

PINTOSMALTO
Pinto see. Then if Pinto Fancy Lady's real husband... that make Pinto King. So treasure is Pinto's.

(Samaritana is struggling to get a heavy treasure sack on the cart. Pintosmalto lifts it on with one hand as if it weighs nothing)

TOLLA
Oh, brother.

QUEEN MENECA
Now, wait a minute...

PINTOSMALTO
So King Pinto take all this and go. And if Fancy Lady bother us ever again, Pinto come back for rest. Maybe take castle too, kick Fancy Lady out, make Betta Queen. Kings do stuff like that, nobody say boo. Or maybe Pinto not need tell anyone he King, maybe Pinto take this stuff, go with Nice Lady, forget all about King thing. Fancy Lady can pick.

QUEEN MENECA
But you... I'm the one that... Curses.

TOLLA
I can't believe we've been thwarted by a guy who can barely conjugate a verb.

BETTA
Uhgg! Everybody on! Baby says it's time to go!

(Pintosmalto hops onto the cart. Betta flips a switch, cart rockets forward. They zoom out the broken wall)

TOLLA
This isn't over yet! I'll free the guards. We can--

QUEEN MENECA

Oh, Tolla, leave it. Let them go. A cheater can hardly complain if she's cheated. Next time I want to decorate my arm, tell me to just get a bangle.

(Exit)

SCENE 15

(Antoniello's house. Iga tends Antoniello who looks deathly ill. Iga see something coming in the distance.)

IGA

Is that... Mistress Betta?

(Antoniello looks up and sees them. He tosses the blanket aside and begins celebrating and hugging Iga, completely healthy again.)

ANTONIELLO

Betta? My child! Oh, Iga, she's returned to us at last!

(Betta, Pintosmalto and Samaritana zoom in, Betta in labor.)

BETTA

Someone hit the brakes! I can't hold it any longer! Ughhhhhaaaaaaaaaaah!

(Samaritana stops the cart so fast the baby shoots out of Betta and into Antoniello's arms. All celebrate and fuss over the baby as they take it offstage.)

TRUFFALDINO

And so Betta returned home with her handmade husband just in time for her Papa to greet his grandchild. Antoniello, from the joy of having them all back safely, was like a healthy lad of fifteen again while Samaritana was welcomed in like a part of the family.

(Betta's workshop, a few months later. As Truffaldino narrates, we see Betta and Pintosmalto working side by

side, the baby strapped to Pintosmalto's chest. All three wear the big protective goggles.)

It would have driven Queen Meneca wild to see how they spent her gold with greasy fingers and shared her treasures with everyone, but she never bothered them again. Together they built a life and, while it wasn't always pretty, pretty isn't everything. And so, side by side, they lived happily ever after.

(Betta and Pintosmalto smile at each other and flip the big switch together. The scene goes dark.)

SCENE 16

(Truffaldino finishes the story and looks up from the book. They are asleep. He carefully puts down the book and starts to sneak out of the room with exaggerated stealth and slowness but just as he reaches the doorway, Nicoletta stirs.)

NICOLETTA
...too quiet... We're awake!

(She wakes violently. Truffaldino freezes, mid sneak. The others rise, groggy.)

LINETTA
That was too close. He nearly got us that time.

RENZA
Not me, I'm not even a little bit...

(very long yawn)

Sleepy.

(She falls back asleep. Linetta shakes her.)

LINETTA
Vigilance, ladies! Be wary of every long blink!

NICOLETTA
Everybody up. Come on. Shake it out.

(The three get up and start to jump around, shaking their limbs and making weird noises to wake themselves up. When they are finished, they stop and regard the still frozen Truffaldino.)

RENZA

Uncle Truff?

(He doesn't move.)
We can see you, you know.

TRUFFALDINO

You're not asleep?

NICOLETTA

Nope.

(With a long frustrated groan, Truffaldino melts into a defeated lump on the bedroom floor.)

LINETTA

Well, that's it. We win. Our Uncle has said Uncle.

RENZA

Yay! Oh, Uncle Truff, we're going to have so much fun! We can play dress up and paint your nails and you can read us a bah-dillion stories while I jump up and down on your nice soft clown belly until the sun rises!

(She pesters him. He plays dead.)

NICOLETTA

Let me see this thing. I'll find us something decent to read this time.

(Nicoletta grabs the book and starts to page through it while Linetta peers over her shoulder. Renza is trying unsuccessfully to move Truffaldino.)

RENZA

Come on, Uncle Truff! You are being like a very squishy unhelpful rock right now.

TRUFFALDINO
I'm playing dead so you'll go away and leave me to my misery. Though I confess it's not really working as well as I'd like.

LINETTA
Wait a moment. Go back... there. That's odd. This story about the three citrons... it's like the one our grandmother always tells about her sisters and the three oranges, isn't it?

NICOLETTA
Huh. Do you think she got it from this book... or the other way around?

RENZA
Let's go downstairs and ask her!

LINETTA
Renza, you tiny genius. It's the perfect excuse to go down and take a peek at the party!

NICOLETTA
Then what are we waiting for? Let's go!

TRUFFALDINO
No no no. You can't go down there. I was supposed to get you to sleep! They'll think I'm washed up for sure! One more story, that's all I need. Where's that book?

> *(He frantically flips through the book. The girls start to leave. To himself, flipping back and forth between stories)*

The three citrons, the three oranges, the merchant with the hydra and the--

RENZA
Bye, Uncle Truff.

TRUFFALDINO
I've got it! Stop right there!

> *(They are gone.)*

Her father really did used to be a bird!

(They peek back in)

LINETTA
What did you--

TRUFFALDINO
It's true. All of it. You want the family stories? The good gossip? Not the guidebook version, the real deal? I got that right here. One more story. Our story. But I'm only telling it if you go back to bed.

(They exchange a look and relent, taking their places on the bed again.)

NICOLETTA
This better be good.

TRUFFALDINO
Once upon a time...

(Bedroom comes apart and assembles into the setting for the final story)

SCENE 17

TRUFFALDINO
This story begins in the dark courtyard of a shadowy castle where few dared to go. Strange sounds echoed from the twisted spires when a peasant girl approached the rusted gate.

RENZA
This one sounds too scary.

LINETTA
I don't see what this has to do with--

(Franceschina enters with a basket. She knocks tentatively on the rusted gate.)

NICOLETTA
Hold on. Is that--

TRUFFALDINO

Shh! No interruptions this time. Just listen.

FRANCESCHINA

Hello? Creonta, your witch...liness? It's me, the butcher's daughter, with your order of... Is anyone here?

> *(She goes to knock again but, before she can touch the gate, it swings open with a long eerie squeal. A scream comes from the castle but is quickly muffled.)*

OK. So it's super creepy here. At least it's not boring like back at the shop. Besides, she's a witch, creepy's her thing. I don't understand why my parents have to be so hexist about it.

> *(With a crash of thunder, the fearsome hag, Creonta, appears from nowhere. Franceschina screams. Creonta cackles.)*

CREONTA

Got you good that time, didn't I?

FRANCESCHINA

Yeah, you did! That was awesome. My heart nearly stopped beating!

CREONTA

Nearly? Must be losing my touch. We'll go for a full skipped beat next time.

FRANCESCHINA

Oh. Well, about that. I'm afraid this is the last delivery.

CREONTA

Nonsense.

FRANCESCHINA

I'm really sorry. My folks were furious when they found out I was coming here. They're just so paranoid about getting mixed up in all this fairy tale stuff. They think I'm going to get turned to stone or cursed to fall in love with a singing apple or something. As if anything that interesting ever happens to me!

CREONTA
But where will I get Sparky her sausages? No one makes them like you do. My little baby loves them so, don't you, girl?

(A roar from offstage.)

FRANCESCHINA
That's a little baby?

CREONTA
Barely a hatchling! Hasn't even grown half her heads yet and still doesn't have the sense not to gobble up her favorites without chewing. She'd choke on those sausages if I didn't cut them up nice--

(A crash offstage. Creonta freezes, sniffing the air.)
Aha! Freed yourselves from my little cage, did you? Never mind, pretties. Creonta loves a chase!

(Creonta disappears as suddenly as she came.)

FRANCESCHINA
Wait! You forgot your... I guess I'll just leave this by the front door so she'll-- Oof!

(She heads towards the castle only to collide with the three frantic princesses who burst out the door. They end up in a heap, the princesses scrambling to right themselves.)

PRINCESS LINETTA
No! Please, we must get away!

PRINCESS NICOLETTA
The witch is nearly upon us!

PRINCESS NINETTA
The gate is open! If we can only reach it in time!

FRANCESCHINA
Whoa! Honest-to-goodness damsels in distress!

(The princesses get to their feet and run towards the

gate but, just as they get there, it slams shut. They pound and pull but it won't budge. With a flash, Creonta returns to the courtyard.)

CREONTA
Surely my little doves didn't think they could fly away that easily?

PRINCESS NINETTA
Please, our father is King of Antipodes. Whatever you desire, he'll grant it.

CREONTA
I know who your father is and he has crossed me for the last time. Now that his precious dolls are mine, I'll have my revenge at last.

PRINCESS LINETTA
No! We beg of you, have mercy!

PRINCESS NICOLETTA
Surely there is some brave hero who will come to our rescue?

(Creonta cackles and conjures a large knife.)

CREONTA
No one's coming, child. You're all alone.

(Franceschina clears her throat.)
Don't be a fool, Franceschina. This affair is none of your concern.

FRANCESCHINA
Well, it's got to be somebody's and there's nobody else here.

CREONTA
You must be joking. What could you possibly do against all this power?

FRANCESCHINA
I could ask you nicely to please not hurt them?

CREONTA
Very well, I won't hurt them.

(Her knife becomes a magic wand.)
I'll keep them for my collection. These three should transform beautifully into flowers or maybe even some fruit. Yes, lovely fresh fruit. A pretty prison of enchantment.

PRINCESS NICOLETTA
No! We'll be frozen in time!

PRINCESS LINETTA
Trapped forever! It's a fate worse than death!

PRINCESS NINETTA
(to Franceschina)
What have you done? You've doomed us!

FRANCESCHINA
I didn't know, I take it back, I--

CREONTA
Some hero. We all have our roles to play and you'd do best to mind yours before you make things any worse.

(She lifts her wand. The princesses cower. Franceschina runs between them.)

FRANCESCHINA
Wait! Stop! You can't just turn people into fruit!

CREONTA
Can't I? Watch me.

TRUFFALDINO
And before the butcher girl could speak again, the witch raised her wand and, with a blast of her magic, poof! She was an orange.

(Creonta raises her wand and zaps Franceschina. Franceschina screams and turns into an orange.)

CREONTA
Stupid girl. You should have stuck to sausages.

(Creonta turns to the princesses.)

PRINCESS NINETTA
No!

PRINCESS LINETTA
Stop!

PRINCESS NICOLETTA
Please...

CREONTA
Enough.

(The princesses scream as Creonta turns them into oranges too. Their three oranges are huddled together while Franceschina's orange stands apart.)

TRUFFALDINO
When the smoke cleared, the princesses were gone and three more oranges stood in their place.

CREONTA
Well, Franceschina, orange you glad you stuck your nose where it didn't belong? You thought you were bored before? Now you've got all of eternity to wish you'd minded your business. Ha!

(She goes back to her castle.)

SCENE 18

TRUFFALDINO
And that was that. The witch continued her wicked ways but the peasant and the princesses could only watch as the world aged around them.

(Many years pass. While the princesses' oranges remain pristine, branches and other random debris fall onto Franceschina's orange, partially obscuring it.)

The days collected up into months which piled up to make years and a big fat nothing changed for the prisoners of the peel. Until, one day, a prince and his dashingly handsome squire battled their way into Creonta's courtyard.

(Prince Tartaglia, his armor improvised from pots and pans, bashes through the gate and makes his way to the three oranges.)

TARTAGLIA

I'm coming, my dearest oranges! There they are!

TRUFFALDINO

But, unfortunately for our heroine, the prince only had love for three oranges.

TARTAGLIA

Squire? A little help?

TRUFFALDINO

Oh! That's me. About two dozen wrinkles ago.

(Truffaldino assumes the role of his younger self, Tartaglia's squire.)

Coming, your highness!

FRANCESCHINA

(muffled, from within orange)
Hey! What about me?

(They don't hear her. Truffaldino helps Tartaglia collect the three oranges and they exit pursued by Creonta.)

CREONTA

No! He's taken them! My oranges! My precious oranges!

(She runs off after them. Lightning streaks across the sky. Creonta screams. Truffaldino pops back in to narrate.)

TRUFFALDINO

As the prince and I took the three oranges away for their happy ending, lightning flashed and the witch let out a terrible scream. Then there was nothing. Soon the only evidence of Creonta's evil reign was a single orange in a ruined courtyard, alone and forgotten. A bit of collateral damage from someone else's fairy tale. But, in time, the magic that bound the orange grew weaker and weaker until...

(Franceschina's orange rocks for a moment until she manages to force a fist through the skin. She battles her way out, kicking her way free of both peel and the debris that's collected on top of it over the years.)

FRANCESCHINA

Finally! Free! I have such a new respect for baby birds. Whoa, what happened here? Where is everybody?

TRUFFALDINO

As she picked through what was left of the castle, she realized decades had passed while she'd been trapped in the orange.

FRANCESCHINA

Everything... everyone I knew. They're all long gone.

TRUFFALDINO

Everything, that is, but...

(Franceschina finds the basket in the remains of her orange.)

FRANCESCHINA

The basket. Of course. None of this would have happened if I'd only... Fine. Lesson learned. From now on, I stick to delivering sausages. Now, where is that witch?

(She grabs her basket and exits)

SCENE 19

TRUFFALDINO

There was a trail of wreckage leading from the ruins and the girl followed it for weeks, figuring if she delivered that last order of sausages, her life would be back on track.

FRANCESCHINA

And I'm not getting sucked into anymore fairy tale trouble, that's for sure.

TRUFFALDINO

But that was harder than she thought. On the first night of her journey, she sheltered in an old barn that turned out to be haunted by a grieving ghost that would not be ignored.

(A ghost appears before Franceschina making spooky sounds that resolve into exaggerated sobbing. She tries to ignore it but it gets up in her face.)

THE GRIEVING GHOST

Boo! Hoo-hoo... Boo-hoo-hoo... Booooo-hoooooo-hoooooo...

FRANCESCHINA

Oh, fine. Uh, don't cry. There there. It'll be OK.

TRUFFALDINO

The spirit was so grateful for her sympathy, it presented her with its hidden treasure.

(Ghost hands her a chest.)

FRANCESCHINA

What's this? Whoa. There's like a fortune in gold coins here. Wait. Let me guess, they're stolen or cursed or magic or some other ghost nonsense, right?

(Ghost dances around mysteriously)

THE GRIEVING GHOST

OooooooooOOOOOOooooooooooOOOOOooooooooOOOOOOOooooooo--

FRANCESCHINA

OK, stop it.

THE GRIEVING GHOST

Boo.

(Crestfallen, the ghost exits.)

TRUFFALDINO
But the girl didn't want to deal with any ghost nonsense so she quickly foisted the treasure off on the first person she saw.

(Bandits enter carrying a wrapped parcel that wiggles and mumbles suspiciously. Franceschina hands one the gold.)

FRANCESCHINA
Here, buddy, free treasure. Have fun with it.

BANDIT
What's this? Gold! A whole mess of it! We're rich!

BANDIT 2
Now we don't even need to bother torturing fancy pants here for the fairy treasure, we got our own! Woohoo!

(They drop their parcel, which emits a muffled "ow", and run off celebrating.)

FRANCESCHINA
There. All done with that. Now to get back on my way.

TRUFFALDINO
She had managed to get rid of the gold alright but, in doing so, she'd accidentally saved a fairy prince from certain death at the hand of bloodthirsty bandits.

FRANCESCHINA
Shut up, I did not.

(A fairy emerges from the parcel)

FAIRY PRINCE
Dearest maiden, you have saved me from a terrible fate!

FRANCESCHINA
Salty ham hocks, seriously?

TRUFFALDINO
Seriously. The prince invited her back to the fairy kingdom where...

FAIRY PRINCE
I will grant you wishes beyond your imagining.

TRUFFALDINO
Which was a pretty sweet deal. But still she refused.

FRANCESCHINA
You know, I'd really love to but... I have to pass... because I've got this thing with these sausages. So... bye.

(She continues on.)

TRUFFALDINO
Yes, no temptation could make her stray from her path. Not even when she came upon the sexiest dude ever leaning against the door of his palace with his shirt all open and his manly man hair flowing and his eyes doing the sexy eye stuff and everything.

(Sexy music as The Sexiest Dude Ever comes into view. A breeze blows open his silk shirt and tosses his impressive locks and as he leans seductively against the doorway of his palace. Think vintage romance novel cover model. Franceschina tries to ignore him.)

THE SEXIEST DUDE EVER
Hello there, m'lady. Won't you rest a moment and partake of the pleasures of my palace?

FRANCESCHINA
La la la, I don't hear anything...

TRUFFALDINO
Even him, she ignored which actually turned out to be for the best because he would have tried to imprison her forever suspended in a web of magic hair that you can only escape with an enchanted dog that can unhinge its jaw to swallow him whole so, honestly, a good call on skipping that one.

FRANCESCHINA
I'm sorry, what? Magic hair?

THE SEXIEST DUDE EVER
Like this! Hair of mine, bind her! You will be mine!

> *(He goes all evil and his hair reaches out like tentacles to bind her.)*

FRANCESCHINA
What the holy hairy what-- Aaaaaaaah!

> *(Franceschina fights off the fierce follicles and hurries offstage. All exit.)*

SCENE 20

(A castle courtyard draped in mourning. A harried Franceschina rushes in.)

TRUFFALDINO
So it went until one day, the trail ended in a strange kingdom all draped in mourning.

> *(She stops a random peasant hurrying past. Random Peasant can be several people with lines divided between them.)*

FRANCESCHINA
Hey! You! Random peasant!

RANDOM PEASANT
Me? But--

FRANCESCHINA
No. I don't want to hear it, OK? I don't care about your talking cat or your giant flea or your brother in law who's a dolphin or whatever fairy tale weirdness you're just dying to drag me into. I am staying out of it. I've got one job and that's finding Creonta so I can finally deliver this basket of sausages.

RANDOM PEASANT
Creonta? The old witch? But she's long dead.

FRANCESCHINA

Creonta's dead? But then how can I--

(Royal guards drag Princess Menechella in kicking and screaming. They chain her to a blood-stained boulder in the center of the castle courtyard. Bones, armor and weapons from previous victims are strew about it.)

MENECHELLA

Let go of me! I don't care if my name came up, the King's daughter shouldn't even be in the drawing in the first place. It's not going to appreciate my royal blood. You might as well just feed it another worthless peasant. Stop this right now!

FRANCESCHINA

What's going on over-- Wait. It's not more fairy tale stuff, is it?

RANDOM PEASANT

No, no. It's nothing like that. They're just feeding the princess to the enchanted dragon who must get a daily sacrifice or it will destroy the entire kingdom.

FRANCESCHINA

How do I keep walking into these situations? Is there a sign on my back or something?

(The guards finish securing the princess. They exit.)

MENECHELLA

No! What are you doing? Don't leave me! I command you to come back here right this instant and untie me! Oh, thank the gods! They're coming back! I knew my father would come to senses.

(Guards enter dragging young Truffaldino who they chain up next to her)

TRUFFALDINO

Now hold on a minute here, fellas. Can't we talk about this?

MENECHELLA

Yes. Much better. Feed it the jester. Nobody will miss him anyway.

TRUFFALDINO
Hey! I'll miss me!

(Once he's secured, the guards leave)

MENECHELLA
Wait! You can't go! You haven't released me. No!

TRUFFALDINO
Princess Menechella. Fancy meeting you here.

MENECHELLA
Shut up, Truffaldino. It's not fair. I did everything I was supposed to. All the stupid prim and proper princess stuff. Years of bows and balls and BS. And for what?

TRUFFALDINO
You? What about me? All I did was tell one, very tasteful, joke about the size of the King's codpiece and--

MENECHELLA
You dunce.

TRUFFALDINO
I'm a clown! What do you expect? I was trying to get him to end my contract. I didn't think he'd end me!

(A terrible roar. Menechella and Truffaldino shriek and clutch each other.)

MENECHELLA
No! I'm too pretty to die!

TRUFFALDINO
Me too!

FRANCESCHINA
It eats one of you every day?

RANDOM PEASANT
Two on cheat days.

(Another roar.)

FRANCESCHINA
Why doesn't someone do something?

RANDOM PEASANT
You know how it is, miss, you've got those sausages. Us, we're bystanders. We stand. By. Like this.

(Peasants begin standing by)

FRANCESCHINA
But you'll eventually all be eaten either way, you might as well... Hello? Hey, don't go all ensemble on me, I'm--

(Two roars at once.)

This is ridiculous! You all played your part to the letter and you're still up to your eyeballs in trouble. It's not like the dragon's all that concerned about shoving its muzzle into someone else's business.

(She wrests an old ax from a skeleton's hand and starts to chop at the chains)

MENECHELLA
Watch it! What are you doing?

FRANCESCHINA
Something. Someone's got to. Hold still!

MENECHELLA
You don't look much like a hero.

TRUFFALDINO
She looks like she's saving our butts. Pretty sure that's the only requirement. But, uh, maybe hurry it up a bit?

FRANCESCHINA
I'm trying! These chains are really thick!

(A chorus of roars. Heavy footsteps approach.)

Oh, bratwurst. I don't suppose it's, like, a small dragon, is it?

TRUFFALDINO
It's huge!

FRANCESCHINA
Of course it is.

MENECHELLA
It's a horrible creature with the wings of a bat and eyes of fire! It's got this huge mouth filled with the sharp teeth of a Corsican hound where every fang drips with acidic drool.

FRANCESCHINA
(awed)
That sounds...

TRUFFALDINO
Yeah and it's got the mewing face of a giant cat with a comb on top like a rooster and the paws of a bear with a tail shaped like a big snake!

FRANCESCHINA
(no longer awed)
...pretty silly, actually. I can't even picture that.

MENECHELLA
You don't need to picture it. It's here!
(She screams as a dragon head comes into view.)

FRANCESCHINA
Wow. It really is goofy looking.

(Dragon roars.)
Aah! No offense! Whoa!

(The dragon lunges for her. A brief battle. After a few close calls, she manages to chop off its head.)
Ha! I did it! I slay the dragon! I wasn't even planning to, I just said to myself, self, it's no different than the block behind the butcher shop back home but with a really really big chicken and I swung and--

(A chorus of angry roars)

There's more than one?

TRUFFALDINO
Not exactly.

(The rest of the dragon enters. It has seven heads total.)

FRANCESCHINA
You went on and on about acid drool and eyes like fire and you didn't think the fact that it's got seven heads worth mentioning?

MENECHELLA
Of course it's got seven heads. What kind of half rate dragon do you think my father would feed me to?

TRUFFALDINO
And that's not all. Look.

(The other heads are reattaching the severed head)

FRANCESCHINA
Seven regenerating heads. Again, something you'd think would make the list of highlights.

(She finally breaks the chains.)

MENECHELLA
Finally! I'm out of here.

FRANCESCHINA
Good plan.

TRUFFALDINO
Screaming and running for my life happen to be specialties of mine.

(Menechella tosses her chains back over Franceschina and Truffaldino. They struggle to untangle themselves)

MENECHELLA
Um, no. You two aren't going anywhere. It has to eat somebody or it'll destroy the whole kingdom. So you're up, unless you want to feed it one of them.

(Bystanders stand by harder)

FRANCESCHINA
What?

TRUFFALDINO
Why you...

MENECHELLA
Loyal subjects, the kingdom will be forever grateful for your brave sacrifice and every year I will light a candle and mourn you for your selfless, blah blah blah, whatever. Later, suckers!

(She runs away. All seven heads roar at once and advance on Franceschina and Truffaldino.)

TRUFFALDINO
Nice dragon...

FRANCESCHINA
Ah ha ha. I hope you're not taking that whole decapitation thing personally. Just a little prank, you know, amongst friends and you've got it back on now so every thing's alright and... Aaaah!

(The dragon goes for them. Franceschina and Truffaldino run around screaming wildly, dodging snapping heads, until the dragon's neck is tied in knots. It wails and struggles to untie itself. They hide behind to catch their breath while it unties themselves.)

Huh. That worked out better than expected.

TRUFFALDINO
Well, it's already untangling itself so now seems like an excellent time to run for our lives and never look back.

FRANCESCHINA
Wait. Princess Menechella's right. If it doesn't eat someone, it'll destroy the whole kingdom.

TRUFFALDINO
I'm not a man of much moral center but I'm going to take a stab here

and say... that's bad and something I totally care about?

(The dragon has untangled itself. Unable to find Franceschina and Truffaldino, it starts to destroy the town. Smoke, fire and chaos. Bystanders scream, scatter and get eaten.)

RANDOM PEASANT
Aaah! Help! Help! It's got me! Noooo!

FRANCESCHINA
Oh, no no. Fatty pork butt, I did it again. I made it worse. Now this whole place is going to be charred rubble and it's all my fault. I should have stuck to sausages. These completely useless sausages.

(She throws her basket of sausages at the dragon. The dragon stops tug of war-ing a random peasant between two of its mouths and turns towards the sausages. After an experimental sniff, the heads begin to gather around the basket, eating voraciously.)

TRUFFALDINO
Hey! You found something it loves to eat more than people! Look at it gobble those sausages up. It's barely taking time to chew.

FRANCESCHINA
Gobbling them up... Sparky? I can't believe it. Sparky, is that you?

(The dragon starts to choke)
Wait a minute, not so fast, those aren't cut up small enough, you'll...

(At once, all heads freeze and then collapse, dead)
...choke.

(Truffaldino gives the dragon an experimental kick)

TRUFFALDINO
Huh. It's dead.

(All the peasants cheer and celebrate.)

RANDOM PEASANT
The dragon's dead! We're saved! Yay! Huzzah! Yayzzah!

FRANCESCHINA
Oh, Sparky. You know, those sausages were for her in the first place. I completed my delivery after all.

TRUFFALDINO
Wow. Just goes to show... something, probably.

FRANCESCHINA
Yup.

RANDOM PEASANT
The dragon has been slain by a true hero at last! As the king decreed, "Whoever should slay the dragon shall be awarded half the kingdom and wed the princess herself."

FRANCESCHINA
I'm not--

RANDOM PEASANT
Oh, it's fine. We're a very progressive kingdom.

FRANCESCHINA
No, I mean, I'm not interested in ruling a kingdom or wedding royalty or anything that sounds like a boring happily ever after just yet. From now on, I'm choosing my own path and seeing what adventures it leads to.

TRUFFALDINO
That's the spirit! And, in my experience, all the best paths lead down to the tavern. I am downright parched after all that excitement. Seeing as you saved me from certain death and all, I suppose I owe you a round. I'm Truffaldino, by the way.

FRANCESCHINA
Franceschina.

TRUFFALDINO
Well, Franny, what do you say?

RANDOM PEASANT
But the King's decree...

FRANCESCHINA
Tell you what. You claim it. Anyone asks, you slew the dragon. Maybe cut off its tongues or something, bring them to the King. Kings like stuff like that.

RANDOM PEASANT
Me? Ruler of the land? Wed to the princess?

FRANCESCHINA
Sure. Why not?

RANDOM PEASANT
I go to claim my destiny!

(Runs off)

TRUFFALDINO
Was that a good idea?

FRANCESCHINA
Sure. Everyone deserves a chance to be the hero.

(As they leave)

TRUFFALDINO
You know, I've done some pretty heroic things myself.

FRANCESCHINA
That so?

TRUFFALDINO
Oh yeah. You ever hear the story of the three oranges?

FRANCESCHINA
Heard it? I was the fourth orange. The one that prince and his fool of a squire left behind to rot when they rescued the other three. What about it?

TRUFFALDINO
Uh, nothing. Nothing at all.

(They exit.)

SCENE 21

(Back in the princess' bedroom, Truffaldino narrates)
And so they lived, well, maybe not always happily--

(An older Franceschina enters)

FRANCESCHINA
But ever after, anyways. Whatever that means.

(The girls are half asleep.)

RENZA
Aunt Franny?

LINETTA
Aunt Franny, you were in the story. The one about grandma and her sisters and the oranges. But how?

NICOLETTA
Does this mean that all those wild stories about our family are actually true?

FRANCESCHINA
Shhh. Go to sleep. I'll explain when you're older.

(She tucks them in. To Truffaldino)
Cheater.

TRUFFALDINO
Hey, that is how it happened! And besides, every bit of that story really is here in this book. Somewhere. A little rearranging, a flip here and there--

FRANCESCHINA
Hey, it worked, that's all that matters.

TRUFFALDINO
They're out?

(She gestures at the girls who are snoring.)

Yessss!

(Truffaldino does an extended celebratory dance that is perfectly silent)

FRANCESCHINA
Are you done?

TRUFFALDINO
Almost.

(Does a little bit more)

FRANCESCHINA
Well, when you're done celebrating, come back down. They've still got some of the cakes out. The toasts went on for ages, everyone was passing out in their pasta. We could all use the famous clown Truffaldino to come liven the evening up again.

TRUFFALDINO
Oh, they're not interested in a dusty old fart like me. They've never even heard of me!

FRANCESCHINA
Hog scraps! You're a classic. When a thing's built well enough, a fresh coat of paint once in a while and it'll stand forever. Go on down there and show them what they've been missing. Just lay off the King cracks this time, pun intended.

TRUFFALDINO
Alright. I'll do it. And you've given me an idea for a whole new routine. Where's that book?

(He grabs the book. He and Franny start to leave.)

FRANCESCHINA
Did the girls give you any trouble?

TRUFFALDINO
Nah. I always knew they'd succumb to my storytelling mastery in the end.

(They are gone. The girls, who were only faking being asleep, hop back up.)

RENZA
Are they gone?

NICOLETTA
Suckers. Leave us out of the fairy tale fun, will they? We'll show them.

LINETTA
Now our adventure starts. Ladies, the party awaits!

(They exit.)

END OF PLAY

~

CURTAIN CALL
My ideal curtain call would be everyone in character at the ball itself. The guests, which are recognizably the characters from the fairy tales, mingle and dance their way through their bows while the young princesses sneak around in the background, evading Truffaldino. When all the other bows are over, the girls step forward to do their bows. Truffaldino catches them at last but they avoid punishment by appealing to his vanity and tricking him into taking a bow himself. Then the four bring everyone together for full company bows.

While this strictly non-compulsory staging may be impossible depending on how you've divided up the roles, consider it inspiration for how to make the bows into a final scene and a farewell to both frame story and tales at once.

Also by Hillary DePiano

HILLARYDEPIANO.COM

FULL LENGTH PLAYS

THE LOVE OF THREE ORANGES
comedy / fantasy /commedia dell'arte
90 to 120 minutes, 8 f, 8 m, 5 any (13-40+ actors possible: 7-20 f, 5-20 m)
A prince is cursed to fall in love with three magical oranges.

THE GREEN BIRD
comedy / fantasy /commedia dell'arte
90 to 120 minutes, 4 m 6 f 3 any (13-40+ actors possible)
Four royals, two clowns and way too many talking statues must unravel the mystery of the green bird before the kingdom is destroyed.

ONE ACT PLAYS

DADDY ISSUES
drama
15 to 20 minutes, 1 female, 1 male, 3 any
A young woman is confronted with the ghost of her past.

POLAR TWILIGHT
comedy / holiday
20 to 25 minutes, 3 f, 3 m (6 actors possible: 0-5 f, 1-6 m)
Everything you know about Santa is wrong and the truth kind of... sucks. Vampire Santa Claus... but in a cute way!

NEW YEAR'S THIEVE
comedy / holiday
30 to 35 minutes, 2 m 3 f 3 any (7 to 10+ actors possible)
Someone's stolen the New Year and the main suspect is... Frosty the coat rack?

WEAK DAYS
comedy
45 to 60 minutes, 6-7 any
All five weekdays play out at simultaneously across the stage in a comic ballet. Winner of The Chameleon Theatre Circle's 16th Annual New Play Contest.

THE LOVE OF THREE ORANGES (ONE ACT VERSION)
comedy / fantasy /commedia dell'arte
35 to 40 minutes, 8 f, 6 m, 4 any (10-30+ actors possible)
A prince is cursed to fall in love with three magical oranges.

THE GREEN BIRD (ONE ACT VERSION)
comedy / fantasy /commedia dell'arte
35 to 45 minutes, 4 m 6 f 3 any (12-40+ actors possible)

Four royals, two clowns, a witch and way too many talking statues must unravel the mystery of the green bird before the witch destroys the kingdom.

SHORT PLAYS (10-15 MINUTES)

THE RAVEN / LENORE
THE THREE LITTLE PIGS AND THE BIG BAD STORM
THE (COMPLETELY INACCURATE) LEGEND OF THE MUMMY WITCH HOUSE
MASKS
THE COMPLETE NOVELS OF JANE AUSTEN: NOW NEW AND IMPROVED!
THREE PADDED WALLS

OTHER FICTION AND NON-FICTION

NANO WHAT NOW?
Finding your editing process, revising your NaNoWriMo book and building a writing career through publishing and beyond.

THE AUTHOR
(award winning novella) You ever get the feeling you don't know which side of the pen you're on?

~

WRITING AS T. W. SELLER
THEWHINESELLER.COM

SELL THEIR STUFF
From eBay Trading Assistants to multichannel seller assistance, your ultimate guide to consignment selling online as a part-time income or full-time business

EBAY MARKETING MAKEOVER
Increase sales and grow traffic to your eBay items by encouraging word of mouth, focusing on your ideal buyers, and optimizing your selling for search and mobile

BEYOND AMAZON, EBAY, AND ETSY
Free and low cost alternative marketplaces, shopping cart solutions and e-commerce storefronts

THE SELLER LEDGER
An auction organizer for selling on eBay

ABOUT THE AUTHOR

Hillary DePiano is a playwright, fiction and non-fiction author best known for fantastically funny fairy tales, surprisingly sweet slapstick and unrelentingly upbeat writing advice. With over two dozen plays for everyone from pre-schoolers and up, she's honored to have had her work performed in schools and theatres around the world.

As the author of the *How to Start Writing* series, she regularly shares advice and pep as a blogger and speaker. Since 2010, Hillary heads the Northeastern New Jersey region for NaNoWriMo.org and works as a volunteer in support of their creative mission. She also writes about eBay, e-commerce, and selling online under the name T. W. Seller (TheWhineSeller.com).

For more information about her books, plays, and blogs or to connect via social media, visit HillaryDePiano.com.

www.ingramcontent.com/pod-product-compliance
Lightning Source LLC
Chambersburg PA
CBHW072036110526
44592CB00012B/1447